PEER REVIEW OF TEACHING

PEER REVIEW OF TEACHING

A Sourcebook

Nancy Van Note Chism

The Ohio State University

With Contributions by
Christine A. Stanley

Foreword by Robert J. Menges

ANKER PUBLISHING COMPANY, INC.
BOLTON, MA

PEER REVIEW OF TEACHING
A Sourcebook

ISBN 1-882982-25-8

Composition by Delaney Design
Cover design by Delaney Design

Anker Publishing Company, Inc.
176 Ballville Road
P.O. Box 249
Bolton, MA 01740-0249

Dedicated to

Robert J. Menges

When I first asked Bob Menges to look at a few pieces I had written on evaluation, he graciously agreed with the special quiet enthusiasm that drew so many people to him. Not only did he respond with thoughtful ideas for the manuscripts, he also continued to send me relevant pieces of literature and to inquire about my progress. Bob served as a mentor for many others in similar fashion. His death in 1998 saddens us, yet his example and written word will continue to inspire us. He wrote the preface to this volume in November 1997. This sourcebook is dedicated to his memory.

About the Author

Nancy Van Note Chism is Director of Faculty and TA Development at The Ohio State University and an adjunct faculty member in the School of Educational Policy and Leadership. Within Ohio State, she coordinates support services for teaching, and teaches research methods and college teaching. She has directed or participated in several major funded projects, including the National Consortium on Preparing Graduate Students as College Teachers (Pew Charitable Trusts), Preparing Future Faculty Program (Pew Charitable Trusts), and the evaluation component of the Gateway Engineering Education Program (National Science Foundation). She is past president of the Professional and Organizational Development Network in Higher Education, an organization of over 1,000 members devoted to improving college teaching.

Chism is the author of 30 edited books, book chapters, and journal articles on teaching and learning in higher education and developing faculty and teaching assistants as teachers, with particular emphasis on multicultural teaching and program evaluation. Chism received a B.A. in English from Fordham University, an M.A.T. in English and Education from Smith College, and a Ph.D. in Educational Policy and Leadership from The Ohio State University.

Contents

Foreword

College and university teaching is most often a solitary activity—my course and my classroom, as we put it. Furthermore, academics are typically left on their own to master the knowledge and the skills that are required to teach well. With peer review, things are very different. Peer review requires collegial conversations about teaching and learning. Peer review promotes examination of our assumptions and rationales for teaching activities. Peer review raises issues about the evidence and standards needed to judge teaching and learning.

In this sourcebook, Nancy Van Note Chism gives us resources to move peer review from the rhetoric of stimulating idea to the reality of good practice. She explicates the meaning of peer review and locates it in relevant theory and research. She provides tools for using peer review: guidelines, protocols, checklists, and rating forms for reviewing course materials, classroom performance, and noncourse teaching activities. And she addresses institution-level issues: policies about peer review; responsibilities of administrators, reviewers, and reviewees; and the components of an effective system for peer review. This sourcebook will find a ready audience as colleges and universities reexamine their teaching missions and their faculty reward systems.

Peer review helps to reinvigorate teaching, whether the purpose is formative or summative. For formative purposes, peer review provides detailed information for appraising one's own work. When reviews are reciprocal, colleagues come to be seen as constructive consultants rather than as potential judges. For summative purposes, peer review enriches the evidence on which decisions about compensation and advancement are made.

Under peer review, teachers and reviewers assume new responsibilities and take new roles. Here are some things expected of teachers who are being reviewed:

- Teachers choose materials that best convey their teaching strengths and their efforts at improvement.
- Teachers reflect on their teaching activities and justify them to reviewers, thus revealing their assumptions and their knowledge of relevant theory and research.

- Teachers defend the consistency between major elements of a course. Are course activities consistent with stated goals? Do procedures for evaluation match course activities and reflect course goals?
- Teachers try to reconcile discrepancies among sources of evidence, including information from the teacher, comments from peers, and evaluations from students.
- Teachers consider whether their approaches and materials deserve dissemination to others.

Here are some things expected of colleagues who serve as reviewers:

- Colleagues decide what aspects of teaching can be best reviewed by peers.
- Colleagues determine how much time and effort are to be devoted to reviewing their colleagues.
- Colleagues seek consensus about the level of achievement that is required for teaching to be judged successful.
- Colleagues confront their own assumptions and practices about teaching and learning, possibly making changes in light of their experiences as reviewers.

We are fortunate to have this timely and comprehensive resource from Nancy Van Note Chism. Her work is certain to stimulate more effective practice of peer review.

Robert J. Menges
Professor of Education and Social Policy
Director of the Center for the Teaching Professions
Northwestern University

(Editor's note: We are honored to have this foreword written by Dr. Menges, as well as his valuable comments on the book as it was being developed, before his death early in 1998.)

Preface

Scholars unanimously agree that evaluating teaching is complex and requires many types and sources of evidence. Faculty quite likely would support this assertion as well. Furthermore, consensus exists among experts that effective evaluation of teaching requires some combination of evidence from the person whose teaching is being evaluated, from that person's students, and from professional colleagues. And while many faculty might agree on the importance of these three sources as well, the prevailing practice in recent years (Seldin, 1998) has been to rely primarily on student ratings of teaching performance, which are distrusted by many, misused routinely, and are only part of the evidence needed for a thorough assessment of teaching. The involvement of peers is too often limited to cursory visits to the classrooms of new faculty or service on a promotion and tenure committee. Real peer review—informed peer judgments about faculty teaching for either improvement or judgment purposes—is too often given short shrift.

Why the lack of emphasis on peer review? This sourcebook will enumerate several reasons but will address one primary reason: the lack of guidance for faculty who wish to do the work of peer review well. *Peer Review of Teaching* attempts to provide a conceptual framework for the use of peer review, a listing of the tasks involved in setting up a peer review system, and practical suggestions and resources that can be adapted by faculty users.

This sourcebook is for administrators who wish to develop a strong peer review component to their system for evaluating and improving teaching and for faculty who will be engaged in the system, both as evaluators and as subjects of evaluation.

ORGANIZATION

Part I: An Overview of Peer Review, contains information on the arguments for peer review and the process of establishing a peer review system. Chapter 1 reviews tenets of effective evaluation of teaching in general, provides a rationale for the use of peer review in evaluating teaching, and discusses issues that arise in considering peer review. Chapter 2 offers suggestions for developing and implementing a system for evaluation of teaching that includes peer review. The role of chairs, colleagues, and peer reviewers are explored in Chapter 3, while Chapter 4 lists the components of a peer review system.

Part II: Resources and Forms, treats several aspects of peer review, outlining considerations that are involved and procedures that can be employed in conducting each type of activity. It contains resources that can be used in reviewing course materials (Chapter 5), classroom performance (Chapter 6), scholarship of teaching and contributions to departmental teaching efforts (Chapter 7), and teaching portfolios (Chapter 8). The intent in Part II is to provide practical formats that can be adopted or adapted for use in actually doing the work of peer review. Part II concludes with a chapter (9) that presents guiding principles for the peer review of teaching, reviews the major points in the book, and offers a bibliography of useful resources.

Peer Review of Teaching: A Sourcebook is offered in the hope that providing examples and suggestions will not reduce the important work of peer review to mere forms or rigid procedures, but will empower faculty to articulate standards, perform their reviews systematically, and perhaps realize that engaging in peer review is an approachable professional task. It is offered as a complement to exciting recent initiatives, such as the Peer Review of Teaching project of the American Association for Higher Education. Such projects take a foundational approach in fostering the notion of teaching as communal work through focusing on peer involvement in ongoing dialogue that probes assumptions, encourages faculty to shares problems and approaches, and—ultimately—creates a culture that supports and sustains good teaching.

ACKNOWLEDGMENTS
Christine Stanley, Associate Director of the Office of Faculty and TA Development, assisted significantly in the compilation of this sourcebook through helping to cull through documents and forms from many locations and proofreading the final draft. Side by side, we developed the forms in Part II, making this process far less tedious than it could have been. I deeply appreciate her encouragement and generous assistance as well as her professional companionship, which I have come to value so highly. Several faculty at The Ohio State University and elsewhere reviewed initial drafts of this sourcebook. I extend special thanks to Faye Dong of the University of Washington, Jane Fraser, formerly of Ohio State, and the late Bob Menges of Northwestern University for their helpful comments.

Nancy Van Note Chism, Director
Office of Faculty and TA Development
The Ohio State University

Part I
An Overview of Peer Review

Chapter 1

Developing a Rationale and Understanding of Peer Review

Evaluation of teaching in higher education has long been the subject of scholarly attention. The literature on one subtopic alone—the use of student ratings forms in the evaluation of teaching—purportedly constitutes the most voluminous component of higher education research. But evaluation is a complex and emotion-charged activity; even though the scholarship is well developed, day-to-day practice continues to struggle.

Within this broad context of teacher evaluation, the status of peer review of teaching is troubled as well. Although colleges and universities have long operated on a tradition of collegial governance, decision-making and mentoring with respect to growth in teaching have created continual anxieties. This chapter will summarize the general implications of the research on evaluation of teaching, then deal with the background for peer review of teaching: the rationale for peer review, issues involved in discussions of peer review of teaching, and the process of implementing a peer review of teaching system.

CENTRAL DISTINCTIONS IN THE EVALUATION OF TEACHING LITERATURE
The substantial body of scholarship on evaluation of teaching includes empirical studies of the validity and reliability of several kinds of evaluation, primarily student ratings, case studies of implementation of programs of teaching evaluation, conceptual work on the assumptions underlying evaluation of teaching, construction of

models, and recommendations for practice. For the purposes of this brief review, the focus will be on one distinction central to this literature—the formative-summative distinction—and generally accepted recommendations in the literature.

The Formative-Summative Distinction

Writing within the context of program evaluation, Michael Scriven (1973) introduced two terms, *formative evaluation* and *summative evaluation*, that have become generally adopted for their usefulness in evaluation of teaching as well. Leading summaries of the state of teacher evaluation, such as the works of Centra (1993a), Braskamp and Ory (1994), and Arreola (1995), all begin with a discussion of these terms, situating them as critical in defining the goals and use of any evaluation activity.

Formative evaluation. Within the context of teacher evaluation, the term *formative evaluation* describes activities that are to provide teachers with information that they can use to improve their teaching. The information is intended for their personal use, rather than for public inspection, and thus is private and confidential. The information should be rich in detail so that teachers can obtain clear insights on the nature of their teaching strengths and weaknesses: Often, text comments or a multitude of very specific rating items tied to course goals and practices will be employed to provide this. Information can come from students, colleagues, administrators, or even through self-reflection or systematic data collection on the part of the teachers themselves, such as classroom research. Formative evaluation is informal, ongoing, and wide-ranging. It is the basis for the development of effective teaching throughout the career.

Summative evaluation. In contrast, summative evaluation of teaching focuses on information needed to make a personnel decision: hiring, promotion, tenure, merit pay. Consequently, the information is for public inspection rather than for the individual faculty member. Since it is not intended to provide rich and detailed data for the improvement of teaching, it is often more general and comparative in nature than data for formative evaluation. Often, quantitative information, such as results of rating or ranking activities, or summary information, such as letters from reviewers, constitute the basis for summative evaluation. The information should provide comparative information as well, enabling the evaluator to determine the quality of the teaching performance with respect to the performance of other peers. Frequently, then, summative data will include norms for a comparison group or statements testifying to the performance with respect to others in the department, college, or field. The attempt is to judge merit or worth to the institution generally. Summative evaluation, in contrast to formative evaluation, is conducted at given intervals, such as annual or promotion and tenure reviews.

Centra (1993a) observes that the critical consideration is actual, rather than intended, use of the information. For example, if data are collected by a teacher for use in shaping a course, but are later submitted as evidence in a promotion and tenure dossier, these should not be thought of as formative. (Unfortunately, however, they are not likely to constitute very useful summative data if they are not global and comparative.) Centra further notes that those who provide formative feedback should not be summative evaluators as well, since the teachers whom they are evaluating will likely be less open and honest with them when they know that these people will later be their judges in a decision-making situation.

Braskamp and Ory (1994, p. 19) summarize some key terms used in portraying each distinction. With formative evaluation of teaching, they associate the terms *individual, career oriented, improvement, development,* and *commitment.* With summative, on the other hand, they associate the terms *institutional, reward oriented, accountability, administration,* and *control.*

Multiple Sources, Methods, Points in Time

The evaluation literature has continually stressed that for evaluations of teaching to be fair, valid, and reliable, multiple sources of information must be engaged, multiple methods must be used to gather data, and the data must be gathered over multiple points in time. Scholars make these distinctions based on which group is the most informed source on the area of teaching to be evaluated and which kinds of data are likely to be most illuminating for a given purpose.

Instructors being evaluated are the primary source of *descriptive* data in that they are the generators of course materials, the teaching philosophy statement and information on number and kind of courses taught, participation in classroom research, leadership in the department or discipline in the area of teaching, thesis and dissertation supervision, mentoring of graduate teachers, and other pertinent descriptions.

Colleagues who are serving as evaluators are best suited to provide *judgmental* response on a person's subject matter expertise, the currency and appropriateness of their teaching materials, their assessment approaches, professional and ethical behavior, and the like. In the role of mentor, colleagues provide feedback in constructive ways; as summative evaluators, they make decisions about comparative quality of the person being evaluated.

Administrators, particularly the department chairperson, can corroborate or supplement descriptions of teaching contributions to the department and to the profession, of professional ethics, thesis or dissertation supervision, the mentoring of graduate teachers, and the like. They can also evaluate the quality of these factors, compared with other faculty in the unit.

Students provide the primary judgmental data about the quality of the teaching strategies employed in courses and their assessment of the personal impact of the teacher on their learning. They can also corroborate or supplement the descriptive data made by the instructor.

Among the methods available for providing evaluative information are the soliciting of narrative documents from any of the above sources (such as the request to prepare a teaching portfolio or letter of recommendation), inspection of materials (such as syllabi or tests), rating or ranking forms (such as student ratings or classroom observation checklists), observations of teaching or committee work performance, counts (such as number of student theses supervised), and telephone or in-person interviews.

Given its nature, formative evaluation should be ongoing; thus these activities should be continual over the instructor's career. For summative evaluation, a systematic schedule outlining when given types of evidence will be collected should be set up, ensuring that a reasonable sampling over the time period being evaluated will be obtained.

Within these general evaluation guidelines, clearly there is a role for peer review, which now becomes the focus of this chapter.

WHY USE PEER REVIEW?

To traditional calls that have advocated the peer review of teaching, several recent arguments have been added that focus on the responsibility of the profession to monitor itself. Foremost among the recent arguments is the call to make teaching "community property." A second rationale is that the evaluation of teaching must reflect the complexity of teaching itself. Third, it is argued that in order for teaching to be valued, there must be an accepted way to judge it.

Teaching as Community Property

The idea of teaching as community property has been promoted vigorously by Lee Shulman of Stanford University through his involvement in a project of the American Association for Higher Education called "From Idea to Prototype: The Peer Review of Teaching" (Hutchings, 1994, 1996a, 1996b). Noting that the culture of teaching in higher education settings has developed a strong norm of privacy, Shulman (1993) points out that such a culture inhibits the growth of what Boyer (1990) has termed "the scholarship of teaching," the thoughtful, problem solving, discipline-based approach to teaching that involves continual reasoning about instructional choices, awareness of the solutions that other scholars have made to key problems in facilitating student learning in the field, and active, ongoing research about the effects of instructor actions on student learning.

Those who advance the notion of teaching as community property talk about various kinds of collaborative activity among faculty, such as team teaching, teaching circles (inquiry groups similar to quality circles in corporate settings), the teaching seminar as a routine part of the interview process, and departmental libraries of syllabi, course materials, and research papers on college teaching (Hutchings, 1996a; Quinlan, 1996). They also argue for a prominent role for peer review of teaching. The rationale is that the faculty must be continually engaged in discussing teaching in order both to nurture new teachers into the community of teacher-scholars and to render the process of making personnel decisions (who gets hired, who gets tenured, who gets merit pay, and the like) more open and more informed by reasoned decisions that consider teaching seriously. The idea is then in the spirit of both continuous quality improvement and the practice of self-regulation within professions.

Teaching as a Scholarly Activity

Making teaching a topic for communal discourse addresses the goal of elevating teaching as a form of scholarship. Just as with other forms of scholarship, public examination, debate, and engagement enriches the inquiry. Scholars and policymakers alike now argue that teaching is too important to leave to individual experimentation and private trial-and-error learning, but must benefit from collective dialogue and sharing of successes and discoveries. Edgerton (AAHE, 1995) uses the analogy of professional sports, pointing out that game tapes are reviewed regularly to assess the effects of various actions and to learn from them. Scholars argue that not only will this collective approach be more effective, but also more efficient, as principles of practice are developed and shared with new professionals.

Inquiry about teaching, especially when it is incorporated into meetings of professional associations, professional journals, and other communication vehicles, will encourage far more systematic research into central issues that have remained relatively unexplored: How do students learn to transfer theoretical information on conservation of energy to a specific case? What teaching strategies can facilitate the process? For which learners? As faculty engage in peer review, these questions come to the fore. Their natural intellectual curiosity then turns to issues that can be addressed for their own teaching and for that of their professional colleagues.

Appropriate Complexity

The importance of the teaching mission to the institution, the situational nature of teaching, and complex web of instructional decisions and effects involved in teaching lead to another argument for peer review of teaching: that any good approach to evaluating teaching will reflect the complexity of teaching itself. Over the years, the evaluation of teaching has gone from a very informal and unarticulated process to one that now relies quite heavily on numeric averages from teaching evaluation instruments that are rated by students (Seldin, 1998). While the inclusion of student ratings has ensured that some data are considered during the process of evaluating teaching, those who study evaluation of teaching are strong in their warnings that the process must rely on multiple sources of evidence from multiple parties (Centra, 1993a; Braskamp & Ory, 1994).

Specifically, experts indicate that while students are the most appropriate judges of day-to-day teacher behaviors and attitudes in the classroom, they are not the most appropriate judges of the accuracy of course content, use of acceptable teaching strategies in the discipline, and the like. For these kinds of judgments, peers are the most appropriate source of information. Sell and Chism (1988) list the following as areas for which peers are the best source of judgments on teaching performance: subject matter expertise, course goals, instructional materials and methods, assessment and grading practices, student achievement, professional and ethical behavior, and thesis supervision. Shulman (AAHE, 1995) distinguishes between judging technical and substantive aspects of teaching, arguing that an intelligent outsider can make determinations about the teacher's speaking skills and the like, but that only a peer can judge whether the teacher is dealing with the subject matter in an accurate and responsible fashion.

Batista (1976, p. 269) provides the following list of faculty behaviors that peers are most suited to judge:

1. Up-to-date knowledge of subject matter
2. Quality of research
3. Quality of publications and papers
4. Knowledge of what must be taught
5. Knowledge and application of the most appropriate or most adequate methodology for teaching specific content areas
6. Knowledge and application of adequate evaluative techniques for the objectives of his/her course(s)
7. Professional behavior according to current ethical standards
8. Institutional and community services
9. Personal and professional attributes
10. Attitude toward and commitment to colleagues, students, and the institution

The recommendation that emerges is for an approach to the evaluation of teaching that mirrors the complexity of teaching itself. The idea of teaching portfolios or dossiers has increasingly become popular, advancing the notion that several types of evidence are important in documenting teaching and that these artifacts make more sense when woven together with a teacher narrative that situates them in the specific context in which they have occurred. Peer review of teaching features prominently in such multidimensional portraits of teaching.

The Value of Teaching

One argument that has traditionally been made for the lack of importance placed on teaching in higher education is that teaching cannot be assessed, therefore it is not valued. Those who make this claim point out that we do not know how to define effective teaching nor how to measure it. Research, however, has consistently shown that there is a great deal of consensus on what characterizes effective teaching. Among those factors that are consistently advanced are subject matter competence, preparation and organization, clarity, enthusiasm, and interpersonal rapport. A review of the data and criteria for exemplary teaching is contained in Menges and Svinicki (1996). Chickering and Gamson's (1987) Principles for Good Practice in Undergraduate Education enumerate seven characteristics that a group of experts identified at a Wingspread Conference:

1. Good practice encourages student-faculty contact.
2. Good practice encourages cooperation among students.
3. Good practice encourages active learning.
4. Good practice gives prompt feedback.
5. Good practice emphasizes time on task.
6. Good practice communicates high expectations.
7. Good practice respects diverse talents and ways of learning.

At the same time, it appears that such lists of characteristics of effective teaching are quite general (as characteristics of effective research would be) and require interpretation and application to specific settings. Judging whether certain sequencing of content or the use of certain metaphors and examples is helpful can be done most effectively by others who understand the discipline. The development of consensus on signs of effective teaching and ways to measure them requires the kind of dialogue among peers that is inherent in peer review of teaching. Shulman (1993) argues that only when teaching becomes "community property" rather than isolated, individual action will it be valued. The communal dialogue that takes place is likely to increase the understanding of the complexity of teaching, thereby engaging the issue of the value of teaching, but it is also likely to generate some practical guidelines for assessing teaching that are owned by the specific teaching community who will use them.

OBJECTIONS TO PEER REVIEW

Even though arguments for peer review of teaching are strong, persistent faculty objections are documented in the literature (Menges, 1991; Pister & Sisson, 1993). These include anxieties about openness and possible threats to academic freedom, the difficulty of defining a peer, problems with finding time to devote to peer review, concerns about the validity and reliability of peer review, and concerns about undesirable aftereffects of the approach.

Opening the Classroom Door

The norms of privacy that have surrounded teaching in recent times are quite powerful. Most teachers, not only those in higher education, have grown accustomed to making teaching decisions without the advice of others and to conducting classes without being observed by others. Although many have experienced perfunctory visits during their first year or two of teaching, such occasions have not been regular and have generally been viewed as "tests" rather than as opportunities to talk about teaching development. The observer has generally been uncomfortable as well, feeling obligated to visit but also having the sense that privacy is being violated.

Such concerns are quite understandable given the norms that have developed, yet several responses can be made. First, equating peer review only with classroom observation is a mistake. As this sourcebook will detail, classroom observation is only one form of peer review—and the one that has traditionally been found least reliable. Second, successful implementation of peer review requires culture change. If the norm of community does not replace the idea of individual teaching entrepreneurs, norms of privacy and competition will prevail. Within the community culture, talks about teaching are continual, not restricted to the visit. Teaching is viewed as inherently interesting and challenging, so the discussion becomes less a critique of individual performance and more an exchange about strategies for solving complex and intriguing problems. If talk of teaching, review of teaching materials, collaboration on teaching, and visits to colleagues' classes characterize a department, concerns about threats to academic freedom are less likely than in settings in which an individual, competitive culture prevails. Further, Edgerton (AAHE, 1995) points out, "With the right 'prompts,' faculty want to talk to colleagues about teaching." In their study of the influence of departmental culture on the ability of faculty to work collaboratively on teaching and learning, Massy, Wilger, and Colbeck (1994) found,

"Faculty in departments that support teaching appear to be less intimidated by peer evaluation than their colleagues in other departments." They point out that junior faculty socialized within a system of peer review are less anxious than "those who have worked for a long time in a system where teaching takes place behind closed doors" (pp. 16-17).

Who Is a Peer?

Over the years, many scholars have wrestled with the question of which colleagues are appropriate peer reviewers. Especially in the case of highly specialized subdisciplines or small departments, it is hard to find a colleague who can provide insights about accuracy and currency of content. For these situations, the best reviewers are likely at another institution, yet the difficulties of distance are then introduced.

Another concern is with the impartiality of peer review, given departmental rivalries and the tendency of human beings to think in terms of their own preferred approach, rather than to value diversity. In an extended analogy, Strenski (1995) compares peer review to the inability of two chefs to agree on the proper way to prepare food. She says, "Ask any instructor about quality of instruction and you will hear an answer inevitably colored by that instructor's own training and model teachers" (p. 34). She cautions that confidence in a peer's opinion must be tempered by knowledge of the philosophical position and pedagogical preferences of the reviewer. Muchinsky (1995) reviews the literature on bias based on friendship and the formation of resulting "mutual admiration societies." He argues that such bias is less likely to crop up when peer review is used formatively than when it is used summatively. In addressing both personal and instructional preference biases, judicious assignment of peer review responsibilities becomes quite important.

The issues involved in identifying a proper peer are substantial. They are not, however, without parallel in the review of research for publication or funding. While one cannot guarantee impartiality, it seems that the only practical course is to work out issues of bias as they occur, understanding that in the long run, some balance will be achieved if the integrity and health of the profession is to prevail. The involvement of multiple reviewers and continuous cycles in peer review also potentially limit the effect of personal bias. Technology will assist in approaching the problem of distance between reviewers. As course materials are available through the Internet and classrooms are more frequently televised or are "virtual," a reviewer at a distance can readily contribute insights concerning a colleague's instructional decisions.

Vulnerability of the Peer Reviewer

A central reason for the reluctance of faculty to serve as peer reviewers—in addition to the personal uneasiness they feel in judging a colleague—is confidentiality. While this is not an issue in formative evaluation, where open and constructive feedback is sought and offered, it becomes quite important when the advancement of a colleague is at stake. While one might expect that professional conduct might encompass having to be open about judgments even when this is personally uncomfortable, such is not always the case. Peer reviewers will be more candid, it is argued, when they are sure that their remarks are anonymous. Yet records of reviews where discrimination is suspected are not considered protected, according to a 1991 Supreme Court ruling *(University of Pennsylvania v. EEOC),* and in locations where an "open records" or "sunshine" law exists, even more access might be available. One possible way to address concerns emanating from lack of confidentiality is to generate collaborative written records in the name of the entire review committee or to present verbal reports to a summarizer.

Vulnerability is also a consideration when colleagues of different ranks are involved in peer review. Again, the purpose of the review makes a difference. When the focus is on formative evaluation, junior faculty might enjoy and benefit from a mutual exchange in which they comment on another's teaching as well as receive feedback. Involving junior faculty in discussing classroom observations and materials prepared by others engages them in teaching issues and helps them to learn from other colleagues. The main concern in these instances is the time commitment required of the reviewer. In the case of summative evaluation, most units stipulate that only senior faculty will serve as reviewers. This protects junior faculty time as well as considers their position with respect to power.

No Time

The most frequent and perhaps most difficult hesitation about peer review is the issue of time. Faculty are feeling more time pressures than ever before, and—given their current responsibilities—they view as unrealistic the expectation that they can regularly review others' course materials, write thoughtful and reflective commentaries following classroom visits, and evaluate extensive portfolios.

There are no easy answers to this issue. The most common response acknowledges that peer review will take time, but argues for the priority of this effort, claiming that the importance of teaching to the institutional mission and the effects of instructional decisions on the learning of students are too great for evaluation of teaching to be less than thorough. For example, the "Pister Report," which summarized recommendations on faculty reward in the University of California system, states, "Documentation and evaluation of meritorious achievement in teaching requires a level of faculty effort well beyond current practice. We urge that peer evaluation of teaching be given the same emphasis now given to peer evaluation of research" (Pister & Sisson, 1993, p. 10).

Others make suggestions for specific time-saving approaches, such as limiting the teaching portfolio to succinct, thoughtful statements on selected key issues (Seldin, 1997) or assigning one or two people on a committee to understand a case in depth and present it to others, as is commonly done in grant proposal meetings, rather than asking each member to attend to all portfolios with equal thoroughness (Bernstein, 1996). A third suggestion is to make periodic decisions about the teaching quality of an individual, as is done for publication of research, rather than delaying any decisions for substantial periods of time. At checkpoints, then, faculty can say that they have had "x" favorable reviews of teaching, much as they can say that they have "x" publications in refereed journals. The summaries of these reviews, rather than the original materials for the reviews (syllabus and the like) can constitute the evidence in the portfolio. Finally, it is argued that lack of regular peer involvement in formative evaluation is an extravagant waste of time when the result is that ineffective teaching is allowed to continue or faculty are ultimately denied tenure. The tradeoff of investing time to avoid this situation is much more productive.

No Standards

Yet another reservation about peer review is the lack of accepted standards for evaluating teaching. Unlike the review of a paper in which the use of a standard statistical procedure can be assessed for its correctness, the review of teaching seems to many to be based on personal preference alone.

As was indicated earlier, the situation is not as fuzzy as some would indicate. Research has isolated effective teaching approaches, yet these are general and rely upon professional judgment for application. The models of the decision-making of the courtroom judge or the connoisseur are more appropriate for the judge of teaching performance than the model of the basketball referee with rulebook. The setting of standards is more fluid and more situational than it is for less complex activities, and the application of the standards requires more judgment. It does not follow, however, that judgments will be totally idiosyncratic and biased. And once again, there are clear parallels in the review of research, where standards are often unarticulated. Arreola's work (1995), in particular, contains practical suggestions for defining standards of performance.

Validity and Reliability Issues

Closely related to the concern about standards, especially when peer review is used for the purpose of making personnel decisions, are anxieties about the validity and reliability of peer review. The internal validity question (Are we measuring what we intend to measure?) does rely on some consensus on what good teaching looks like in the specific situation at hand. In addition, however, the internal validity question engages the question of inquiry method. Since recommendations on the implementation of peer review embed the approach within a design that not only involves consensus on standards, but advocates multiple reviewers, multiple methods, and sustained engagement, it can readily be seen that such a system has distinct validity advantages to the single source (student ratings) approach or the "gut feeling" approach.

Concerns about reliability (Are we measuring consistently and accurately?) are supported in the scholarly literature, especially the research on classroom observation. For example, several scholars (Ceci & Peters, 1982; Centra, 1975; Cohen & McKeachie, 1980; Feldman, 1989; and Kane & Lawler, 1978) have found that peer reviewers disagreed substantially on their assessments of the same classroom teaching performance. Centra (1993b) recently found a high level of disagreement on judgments of portfolios as well. The problems appear to be connected with three key factors: lack of consensus on standards for judgment, lack of observation or content analysis skills on the part of the reviewers, and lack of systematic process and documentation. All of these issues are not insurmountable, but clearly must be addressed in an implementation plan to ensure the success of peer review.

Undesirable Aftereffects

Some concerns about peer review, especially for promotion and tenure decisions, focus on undesirable outcomes, such as divisiveness within the department. The argument is that confidentiality of the reviewer will be difficult to preserve and the resulting openness will make the reviewer more cautious about negative judgments and the colleague under review more likely to take such judgments personally. While the most long-term response to this fear is that the culture must change to support open, collective inquiry on teaching and thus eliminate the desire for secrecy, the short-term response is that multiple peer reviewers must be involved in any one case. The resulting decision is collectively rendered, rather than the personal judgment of one person.

A second concern is that, when used for decisions about tenure or merit increases, peer review of teaching will reduce risk-taking in teaching: Faculty will use only traditional strategies because they fear that initial failures or adjustments necessary to test innovative techniques will be documented, tainting their review. Initial attempts toward innovative teaching often misfire and require a period of fine tuning; therefore, judgments of teaching must be sensitive to a developmental pattern that involves cycles of experimentation. In the case of peer review for ongoing improvement purposes, information on this pattern is imperative, but it is also helpful in the case of peer review for personnel decisions. Indeed, it would be difficult to show improvement in teaching unless there is some evidence that undesirable situations have been identified and worked through. Documentation of this process should be an essential part of a teaching portfolio. The absence of any experimentation, similarly, should be cause for concern. Faculty need to understand these expectations of the review process in order to feel comfortable about attempts to innovate.

Third is the apprehension that legal challenges to personnel decisions will increase with the use of peer review of teaching. Since the existing system for evaluating teaching is generally based on student ratings data and peer opinion, there does not seem to be a logical basis that a system that is based on multiple sources and kinds of data, including peer review information, would be more vulnerable than the current system. In fact, when peer review of teaching is implemented systematically, it provides more justification and documentation for a decision.

A good system for the evaluation of teaching that incorporates peer review must address the objections that are raised to the satisfaction of the faculty community. The first step is to invest sufficient effort in setting up a good system.

REFERENCES

American Association for Higher Education. (1995). *From idea to prototype: The peer review of teaching (a project workbook).* Washington, DC: AAHE.

Arreola, R. (1995). *Developing a comprehensive faculty evaluation system: A handbook for college faculty and administrators on designing and operating a comprehensive faculty evaluation system.* Bolton, MA: Anker.

Batista, E. (1976). The place of colleague evaluation in the appraisal of college teaching: A review of the literature. *Research in Higher Education, 4,* 257-271.

Bernstein, D. (1996). A departmental system for balancing the development and evaluation of college teaching. *Innovative Higher Education, 20,* 241-247.

Boyer, E. (1990). *Scholarship reconsidered: Priorities of the professoriate.* Princeton, NJ: The Carnegie Foundation.

Braskamp, L., & Ory, J. (1994). *Assessing faculty work: Enhancing individual and institutional performance.* San Francisco, CA: Jossey-Bass.

Ceci, S., & Peters, D. (1982). Peer review: A study of reliability. *Change, 14* (6), 44-48.

Centra, J. (1975). Colleagues as raters of classroom instruction. *Journal of Higher Education, 46,* 327-337.

Centra, J. (1993a). *Reflective faculty evaluation: Enhancing teaching and determining faculty effectiveness.* San Francisco, CA: Jossey-Bass.

Centra, J. (1993b). *Use of teaching portfolios and student evaluation for summative purposes.* Paper presented at the annual meeting of the American Educational Research Association, Atlanta, GA. ED 358 133.

Chickering, A., & Gamson, Z. (1987). Seven principles for good practice in higher education. *AAHE Bulletin, 39* (7), 3-7.

Cohen, P., & McKeachie, W. (1980). The role of colleagues in the evaluation of college teaching. *Improving College and University Teaching, 28* (4), 147-154.

Feldman, K. (1989). Instructional effectiveness of college teachers as judged by teachers themselves, current and former students, colleagues, administrators, and external (neutral) observers. *Research in Higher Education, 30* (2), 137-94.

Hutchings, P. (1994). Peer review of teaching: From idea to prototype. *AAHE Bulletin, 47* (3), 3-7.

Hutchings, P. (1996a). *Making teaching community property: A menu for peer collaboration and peer review*. Washington, DC: AAHE.

Hutchings, P. (1996b). The peer review of teaching: Progress, issues, prospects. *Innovative Higher Education, 20,* 221-234.

Kane, J., & Lawler, E. (1978). Methods of peer assessment. *Psychological Bulletin, 85,* 555-586.

Massy, W., Wilger, A., & Colbeck, C. (1994). Overcoming "hollowed" collegiality. *Change, 26* (4), 11-20.

Menges, R. (1991). *Why hasn't peer evaluation of college teaching caught on?* Paper presented at the annual meeting of the American Educational Research Association, Chicago, IL. ED 337 106.

Menges, R., & Svinicki, M. (1996). *Honoring exemplary teaching.* New Directions for Teaching and Learning, *65.* San Francisco, CA: Jossey-Bass.

Muchinsky, P. (1995). Peer review of teaching: Lessons learned from military and industrial research on peer assessment. *Journal of Excellence in College Teaching, 6* (3), 17-30.

Pister, K., & Sisson, R. (1993). *The Pister Report: Lessons learned—the aftermath of the report of the task force on faculty roles and rewards in the University of California.* Presented at the first AAHE Conference on Faculty Roles and Rewards, San Antonio, TX.

Quinlan, K. (1996). Involving peers in the evaluation and improvement of teaching: A menu of strategies. *Innovative Higher Education, 20,* 299-307.

Scriven, M. (1973). The methodology of evaluation. In B. Worthen & J. Sanders (Eds.), *Educational evaluation: Theory and practice* (pp. 60-104). Belmont, CA: Wadsworth.

Seldin, P. (1997). *The teaching portfolio: A practical guide to improved performance and promotion/tenure decisions* (2nd ed.). Bolton, MA: Anker.

Seldin, P. (1998). How colleges evaluate teaching: 1988 vs. 1998. *AAHE Bulletin, 50* (7), 3-7.

Sell, G., & Chism, N. (1988). *Assessing teaching effectiveness for promotion and tenure: A compendium of reference materials.* Columbus, OH: The Ohio State University Center for Teaching Excellence.

Shulman, L. (1993). Teaching as community property: Putting an end to pedagogical solitude. *Change, 25* (6), 6-7.

Strenski, E. (1995). Two cheers for peer review: Problems of definition, interpretation, and appropriate function. *Journal of Excellence in College Teaching, 6* (3), 31-49.

Chapter 2

Setting Up a System for Peer Review

In order to be effective, peer review of teaching must be situated within a system that emphasizes the value of teaching to the institution and articulates a thoughtful and comprehensive approach to the evaluation of teaching. Developing and implementing such a system requires leadership at each administrative level: institution, college, and department.

INSTITUTIONAL LEADERSHIP

A major study of faculty and administrator perceptions on the value placed on teaching at major universities found that faculty think that administrators place less value on teaching than the faculty do (Gray, Diamond, & Adam, 1996). Interestingly, individual faculty members surveyed in this study also think that they place more value on teaching than their colleagues do. In the same survey, administrators said that they place more value on teaching than faculty perceive them to do. So the picture that emerges is of contrasting perceptions and confused expectations all around. Faculty have a hard time believing administrative pronouncements about the value placed on teaching, and administrators think that faculty themselves are pressuring their colleagues to place less value on teaching than on research. The first step to implementing a peer review of teaching system is clarifying this value question, not only with pronouncements, but with actions. In the case of peer review, actions center on requiring documentation of positive peer review for personnel decisions and consistently making judgments based on the total evidence, including peer review.

Since teaching is situational, leadership at the institutional level must provide broad guidelines to allow for adaptation at the department level. Among the principles that can be enunciated are:

- Evaluation of teaching must be done in a systematic, thoughtful manner.
- Provisions must be made for both formative evaluation (for improvement) and summative evaluation (for personnel decisions).
- Evaluation of teaching for personnel decisions must be multidimensional and include evidence from multiple sources (the faculty member, students, peers, and relevant others), multiple kinds of evidence (ratings, reflective statements, narrative appraisals, artifacts of teaching such as syllabi), and be done over an extended period of time. The submitted evidence must indicate the context of the teaching and comparative information on expectations for faculty teaching in the field.
- Evaluation of teaching must be appropriate to the teaching context, and clear guidelines must be accessible to all. Departments must invest time in developing and announcing their approach to evaluation of teaching and the place of peer review within that system. A written document describing that system should be on file at the institutional level as well as at the college and departmental levels.

Richlin and Manning (1995a) note that systems must also be 1) safe, in that they must ensure that outcomes will not be arbitrary; 2) manageable, given the resources of the unit; and 3) compliant with environmental demands for accountability and quality as well as internal unit needs.

At the institutional level, oversight should be exercised, focused on ensuring that departments develop and document systems for the evaluation of teaching that are in keeping with these principles.

Resources, such as expert help for departments developing a system, should also be provided from the institutional level.

COLLEGE LEADERSHIP

In situations in which there is a college structure under the institutional level, it is incumbent upon the college administration to reinforce the principles and help departments to adapt them to their particular teaching situations. It is also important that when personnel reviews are conducted at the college level, the reviewers operate within a framework that is consistent with announced values and principles for evaluation. Colleges can also provide leadership for formative activities, including mentoring programs, classroom feedback services, and various kinds of teaching discussions.

DEPARTMENTAL LEADERSHIP

Much of the work supporting the development of an evaluation of teaching system that includes peer review needs to occur at the departmental level. The articulated institutional value on teaching is operationalized within the department. If resources and rewards are not allocated in appropriate proportion to the value on teaching, the discrepancy will undermine any pronouncements and documentation. It may help to appoint a strong teaching committee to help ensure that decision-making remains consistent with principles.

Developing a Statement

In developing a system for the evaluation of teaching, particularly one that includes provisions for peer review, the ideal starting place is an extended and serious departmental conversation that addresses the following questions (sets of questions are also contained in AAHE, 1995, and Richlin & Manning, 1995b):

1. Who can benefit from evaluation of teaching in this department? (Should it be restricted to pretenure faculty, or should senior faculty be included as well?)
2. How do we view the relation between the two purposes of evaluation? (Improvement purposes versus documentation for personnel decisions such as merit increases, promotion and tenure?) Should we set up separate systems or blend them?
3. What areas of teaching will we assess?
4. How specific can we be in articulating our standards in such areas as:

- Effective course design
- Effective classroom performance
- Effective course materials (syllabi, handouts, tests, coursepacks)
- Effective contributions to teaching within the department
- Effective contributions to teaching in the discipline

5. What recommendations will we make on procedures for collecting evidence for those areas of teaching performance that we want to assess?
6. How will we provide resources to accomplish systematic evaluation of teaching?
7. How will we document and communicate our plan?
8. How will we monitor our plan?
9. How often should we revise our plan?

Such a conversation cannot take place in one sitting. Depending on the departmental situation, the chair might appoint a committee to hold preliminary discussions and bring recommendations to others, or small task groups can be assigned responsibility for exploring certain questions and making recommendations for those areas. Eventually, however, a discussion involving all members of the department should be held, not only to seek input but also to build ownership. Since evaluation of teaching is a sensitive issue, help from a facilitator from another department or someone outside the department structure might be useful. The discussions have the potential for initiating critical reflections on teaching that are developmental in themselves and will help to establish the idea of "teaching as community property."

Although he notes that there is often resistance, Arreola (1995) observes that the time committed to initial planning will reap results in the efficiency and effectiveness of the process later. He points out that if a major, thoughtful discussion results in clear, accepted standards, applying those standards to particular cases later is not a daunting or mysterious task. The raw materials upon which the review is based will not need to be reviewed again at subsequent levels, when the first-level peer review results can be used instead, with considerable reduction in amount of documentation.

The resources that follow in this sourcebook might be a helpful starting point for the discussion of standards. They should be adapted and modified as the faculty sees fit in order to reflect its notions of the standards appropriate for the field and the methods of evaluation that are most useful in assessing teaching. If the resources provoke considerable dissension, however, it might be best to start with a blank slate and generate standards from the group.

The main goal of the process is to develop a clear statement of how teaching will be evaluated within the department both formatively and summatively. (An example of such a statement is at the end of this chapter.) Such a system should not be so perfunctory that it does not reflect the complexity of teaching, but it must be realistic in the amount of effort and expertise that its use demands. It must be consistent with the principles articulated at the institutional and college levels.

The statement should be practical. It should be accompanied by resources, such as checklists or examples of a good narrative statement evaluating course materials and the like. It should contain "how to" advice as well as principles. Particularly in the area of peer review, few resources have been developed in the past, and the process has remained mysterious and idiosyncratic.

If the faculty has been involved in developing the departmental approach to the evaluation of teaching, obtaining consensus on the final plan should not be difficult. If the large size of a department or the process used to arrive at a plan has precluded broad involvement, a final step in arriving at a plan is to make sure that faculty understand the plan and support it. An additional stage of dissemination, discussion, and modification might be necessary.

Finally, the statement and accompanying resources should be disseminated within the department and placed on file at the college and institutional levels.

Implementing the System

Once the plan has been communicated and has the support of the faculty, it is important to think about how to support its accomplishment, monitor progress and problems, and revise it as necessary. In small departments, the chairperson might be able to assume these responsibilities and achieve them informally. In larger departments, an oversight committee might be assigned responsibility to assess implementation.

Preparing colleagues. One of the most overlooked aspects of incorporating peer review into the evaluation of teaching is preparing colleagues to assess each other's teaching.

Paying explicit attention to this at the start will reap rewards as the process unfolds. Organizing sessions to practice with checklists or "calibrate" by discussing how each would rate a given course material will help faculty to raise questions and understand how to approach this kind of assessment. Practicing giving formative feedback to colleagues in helpful ways can enhance its effectiveness. Reviewing sample materials or videotapes of classroom teaching can stimulate discussion among faculty on how to apply the standards that have been developed and how to use the resources that have been designed. Often, such sessions can be facilitated by a teaching consultant, a skilled member of the department, or a faculty member from another department. Making it clear that part of the assessment of teaching is assessing one's contributions as a peer reviewer will help to reinforce the investment made in developing one's skills.

Distributing responsibilities. In the particular case of peer review, the distribution of responsibilities might be an issue. Assigning colleagues to provide feedback for improvement and to document teaching performance for personnel decisions must be done carefully so that appropriate and helpful assignments are made and time demands are shared equitably. Often a handful of faculty members most skilled in this area are asked to shoulder a disproportionate share of the time commitment. These individuals might be asked to help other faculty learn to become skilled developers of other faculty talent as well. Inevitably, the question of conflict of responsibilities between a peer who is assigned both formative and summative functions occurs. In the best of circumstances, the formative and summative information should flow together: Information on what improvements are needed can be tracked to show improvement. Most parties, however, prefer to separate these functions so that the mentor is not the judge. Arrangements for accomplishing this division of responsibilities will need to be made, often by using peers outside the department. Muchinsky (1995) and others observe that when content is being judged, it is best to choose peer reviewers based on knowledge of the discipline, but when general teaching performance is being assessed, it is appropriate, perhaps even desirable, that the reviewers be unfamiliar with the subject so that they can make an assessment based on the role of the "naive learner." Outside peers will have to understand the evaluation system as well.

Monitoring the process. Monitoring the thoroughness, timeliness, and fairness of the system will also be important. At the time of annual reviews, it should be clear whether or not the appropriate activities and their documentation are occurring. The chair or oversight committee can monitor the situation and call for change. If the situation warrants it, the department can be asked to consider changes or to help troubleshoot the situation. Provisions should be made for periodic reexamination of the evaluation of teaching plan and for its revision.

Additional discussions of the development and implementation of peer review systems for both formative and summative purposes are contained in Hutchings (1996a), Bernstein (1996), and Quinlan (1996). Workbooks for devising systems have been developed by the American Association for Higher Education (1995) and Richlin and Manning (1995b).

Example of a Statement

In his discussion of the case of one department's experience in developing and implementing a peer review system, Nordstrom (1995) includes the statement that resulted.

A Protocol for a Peer Review Program in the Department of Marine and Coastal Sciences at Rutgers University

1. The department should have an established process of peer review for faculty to use in improving their course instruction and enhancing their chances of success in personnel decisions.
2. Peer review is strongly recommended, but not required, for all courses an instructor teaches.
3. Peer review should be considered only one of many different ways that teaching effectiveness can be evaluated.
4. The emphasis on peer review should be on its value to the instructor, the process should be instructor-driven, and the results should be the property of the instructor.
5. The review should involve using standardized, faculty-approved worksheets: one for review of course materials and one for review of classroom instruction.
6. The worksheets should be constructed so the reviewers can obtain insight along with the instructor being reviewed.

7. Prompts may be included in the worksheets to ensure that the instructor and the reviewers consider important aspects of a teaching program.

8. The worksheets should be updated periodically to reflect changing departmental goals and conceptions of student learning and to make them compatible with new initiatives for improving teaching effectiveness.

9. The review should be conducted no earlier than midterm if the course is being offered for the first time.

10. The instructor should provide copies of the syllabus and all handouts, assignments, and exams for the review of course materials. A copy of the documentation used for course approval and the description of the course in the university catalog should also be available.

11. At least two in-class observations are suggested for review of classroom instruction.

12. A meeting to discuss teaching issues of mutual interest should be held as part of both the review of course materials and the review of classroom instruction. The meetings also allow the instructor to elaborate on teaching goals and strategies and to rebut negative comments.

13. If the review is to be used in making a personnel decision, the comments on the reviewers' worksheets should be finalized only after these meetings

14. Use of peer review results in making a personnel decision should occur via the instructor to the maximum extent possible (e.g., through incorporation into a teaching portfolio).

15. Peer reviews for personnel decisions and course improvement should not be conducted simultaneously, but the same reviewer worksheets should be used for both types of review.

16. An individual conducting a review for a personnel decision should have experience in reviewing other courses, should have taught a course at the same level as the course being reviewed, and should be open to alternative teaching strategies and conceptions of student learning.

17. The opportunity for remedial action, through subsequent reviews initiated by the instructor, must be made available following negative reviews made for a personnel decision.

18. Subject to approval by instructors, worksheets may be synthesized to identify department-wide teaching and curricular problems needing remediation.

19. A departmental library of teaching resources should be maintained for faculty use.

Characteristics of an Effective Peer Review Process

In summary, the following are characteristics of an effective peer review process:

1. It provides for both formative feedback and summative decision-making.
2. Peer reviewers understand their task and are well prepared to accomplish it.
3. Trust and confidence in the process is exhibited by all parties.
4. Ongoing departmental efforts are invested in improving the peer review process.
5. Peer review assignments are made in ways that are likely to result in helpful collaborations.
6. Peer review is a valued process within the department.
7. Parties are cooperative and timely in accomplishing peer review tasks.

REFERENCES

American Association for Higher Education. (1995). *From idea to prototype: The peer review of teaching (a project workbook).* Washington, DC: American Association for Higher Education.

Arreola, R. (1995). *Developing a comprehensive faculty evaluation system: A handbook for college faculty and administrators on designing and operating a comprehensive faculty evaluation system.* Bolton, MA: Anker.

Bernstein, D. (1996). A departmental system for balancing the development and evaluation of college teaching. *Innovative Higher Education, 20,* 241-247.

Gray, P., Diamond, R., & Adam, B. (1996). *A national study on the relative importance of research and undergraduate teaching at colleges and universities.* Syracuse, NY: Syracuse University Center for Instructional Development.

Hutchings, P. (1996a). *Making teaching community property: A menu for peer collaboration and peer review.* Washington, DC: American Association for Higher Education.

Muchinsky, P. (1995). Peer review of teaching: Lessons learned from military and industrial research on peer assessment. *Journal on Excellence in College Teaching, 6* (3), 17-30.

Nordstrom, K. (1995). Multiple-purpose use of a peer review of course instruction program in a multidisciplinary university department. *Journal on Excellence in College Teaching, 6* (3), 125-144.

Quinlan, K. (1996). Involving peers in the evaluation and improvement of teaching: A menu of strategies. *Innovative Higher Education, 20,* 299-307.

Richlin, L., & Manning, B. (1995a). Evaluating college and university teaching: Principles and decisions for designing a workable system. *Journal on Excellence in College Teaching, 6* (3), 3-15.

Richlin, L., & Manning, B. (1995b). *Improving a college-university teaching evaluation system: A comprehensive, developmental curriculum for faculty and administrators* (2nd ed.). Pittsburgh, PA: Alliance Publishers.

Chapter 3

Understanding Roles and Goals of a Peer Review System

Initial clarity about the reasons for engaging in peer review and expectations for the role that is to be played by each person in an academic unit is a hallmark of good systems of peer review. This chapter will treat the topics of roles and goals.

ROLES

Effective peer review of teaching involves the collaboration of several parties, including the chairperson, colleague being reviewed, and peer reviewer. Each has a role in the process and can contribute different things.

The Department Chair

The chair is responsible for creating a climate that values peer review. This can only be situated within a climate that values teaching and therefore supports continual efforts to develop and evaluate teaching. Department chairs can create a supportive climate in a variety of ways.

Assuming intellectual leadership for the effort. Effective chairpersons are knowledgeable about the literature on good teaching, on teaching assessment, and on teaching improvement. Chairs can show faculty that teaching can be analyzed and assessed in valid and reliable ways. They can convene meetings to set up a peer review system that is thorough and informed.

Communicating high expectations for teaching and peer review. Through pronouncements and actions, the chair can alert faculty to the seriousness with which teaching is taken in the department. Faculty can be continually informed that peer review is expected and should receive their full attention. Although concerns about how much time goes into effective peer review are important, the department chair should communicate a clear sense of the high priority that must be placed on this function.

Making teaching public. Chairpersons can work to ensure that there is ongoing public dialogue on teaching at department meetings, workshops, and other occasions. The chair can strive to be personally accessible for discussion of teaching issues. Peer review then becomes a natural part of the dialogue.

Providing sufficient resources for peer review. The way in which the chairperson provides leadership in selecting new faculty, allocating rewards, and making assignments clearly indicates a stance on teaching. Chairpersons can be on the alert for ways in which they can provide time and resources for serious peer review.

Assisting in the assignment of peers. The chair can oversee the process of assigning peer reviewers to assess the work of a given faculty member. This task might be accomplished by delegating it to a faculty committee, by direct nomination or appointment by the chair, or whatever arrangements make sense in the department. The chair can help to ensure fair and helpful reviews by being alert to interpersonal conflicts, philosophical differences, and other conditions among the teaching staff that might get in the way of good peer review.

Taking part in the peer review process. The chair can set an example by being personally involved in formative peer review, observing classes of faculty, reviewing their materials and the like, and providing feedback. The chair plays an important role in summative peer review, setting the tone of the review committee and encouraging it to make decisions based on careful analysis of the information that is available.

Providing guidance to peer reviewers. The chair can help to arbitrate differences among peers that arise during the review process and can intervene as necessary to help provide perspective on differences among faculty, standards for judgment, and comparisons.

The Colleague Being Reviewed

Teachers being evaluated can provide important contextual information needed during the peer review process. They can also initiate actions for formative review, inviting peers to provide feedback on course materials, classroom performance, or other aspects of teaching.

For formative purposes, teachers can provide, during preobservation conferences or other interchanges, information concerning appropriate materials about the course, the instructional strategies, the level of students taking the course, and other contextual information that can be helpful to the reviewer.

The role of the colleague in summative peer review is to assemble the best evidence of teaching available and to provide additional evidence at the request of the committee. Such evidence includes representative samples of course materials, a chronological record of teaching responsibilities, a list of publications and presentations on teaching, student evaluations of teaching, records of consultations or feedback from sources outside the department, and other things required by the department or institution in a dossier.

The Peer Reviewer

The peer reviewer can be developer, information gatherer, or judge. In the role of developer, he or she is supportive, assisting the colleague in teaching development, and offering suggestions for change and improvement. As information gatherer, the role is one of collecting appropriate information to be used formatively or summatively in the peer review process. As a judge, the peer reviewer evaluates sources of data on teaching that are used for personnel decisions. Ideally, the peer reviewer will play only one of these roles for any given faculty colleague, separating the formative and summative functions.

The role of the reviewer in formative peer review is to gather appropriate information from the colleague during preobservation conferences or other interchanges concerning appropriate materials about the courses taught, the instructional strategies, the level of students taking the courses, and other contextual information that can be helpful to the reviewer. Once information is gathered, the peer reviewer has the responsibility to view the teaching products or performance in light of the context and make helpful comments and suggestions to the colleague in follow-up sessions.

The role of the reviewer in summative peer review is to collect that information that the reviewer is best qualified to judge. A review of the literature on the role of colleagues in peer review of teaching (Cohen & McKeachie, 1980) states that peer reviewers are in an ideal position to judge course content and design, materials, and instruments used to assess student achievement. Peers are also the appropriate judges of the products of the scholarship of teaching and the colleague's contributions to teaching development in the department, college, institution, or profession. The peer reviewer should assess the evidence in these areas according to departmental and institutional standards and render fair evaluations based on these standards.

GOALS

As has been stressed throughout this sourcebook, it is important to adopt separate procedures for formative and summative peer review. Formative peer review is intended for improvement of the person being reviewed, and the emphasis is on constructive feedback. Summative peer review is intended to be the basis for a personnel decision, such as promotion, tenure, or merit pay, and the emphasis is on making fair judgments.

Formative Peer Review: Providing Constructive Feedback

In providing a colleague with feedback for improvement following a class observation, review of materials, or other peer review activity, it is helpful to consider the following:

- Authentic feedback is built on a relationship of trust, honesty, and genuine concern for the individual. Rivalries, flattery, and condescension get in the way of effective dialogue.
- Descriptive information provides the colleague with concrete details on which decisions for change can be based. It allows the colleague to consider whether the description fits his or her intentions and to make adjustments if not. (Example: "Ninety percent of the class time was devoted to teacher

talk," or "The syllabus never lists the causes of the French Revolution as a topic to be treated.")

• A focus on behavior rather than personal attributes isolates those things that can be changed more easily and avoids associating personal blame with problems. (Example: It is better to say "I noticed that the students appeared tired when they did not have a break during the three-hour class" than "You are really inconsiderate.")

• Feedback that is rooted in the needs of the colleague is most helpful. It is responsive to the self-identified questions that the colleague has, to the stage of his or her career, and to the individual's capacity to absorb information and make necessary adjustments. Reviewers should encourage colleagues to identify the questions and concerns that they themselves have. (Example: "In looking over this test, what items do you have uncertainties about?" "Would you like suggestions for redoing the whole format or just changes on specific items?")

• Peer review activities should be followed by prompt feedback. While recall of details is fresh and colleague expectation for response is high, dialogue between the peer reviewer and colleague should occur. It is often helpful to schedule a meeting time for this exchange at the same time when the initial peer review activity is scheduled.

• Checking periodically during a feedback session to hear how comments are being heard and interpreted is helpful. (Example: "Can you summarize the main points I have made about what I saw in the laboratory exercise?")

• If multiple peer reviewers are involved, it is useful to check for agreement on specific observations or advice. (Example: "Did anyone else notice that students' attention levels lagged after the first fifteen minutes of lecture?" "Do you find the layout of these handouts confusing?")

• Feedback that is forward-looking helps the colleague to go beyond the peer review activity. When suggestions for specific change or a plan for development are part of a feedback session, the colleague has identified a practical outcome. (Example: "I would suggest that you limit the content of your overhead transparencies and use a bigger, bolder font so that students stop complaining that they cannot see them or copy them down quickly.")

Summative Peer Review: Rendering Judgments

When peer review of teaching is performed for summative purposes, several guidelines are relevant:

- Reviewers should make sure that they are appropriate judges. If there are conflicts of interest, if the teaching is being done in a specialized area that is unfamiliar to the reviewer, if there are longstanding personality conflicts between the reviewer and the colleague being reviewed or the reviewer and other peers on a review committee, or if there are other compelling reasons why the reviewer cannot do a thorough and fair job, the reviewer should request to be excused from the review.

- Adequate conditions should be available for summative peer review of teaching. If there is an attitude of distrust, insufficient time, or lack of evidence, these must be addressed before a good review is possible. If lead time has been lacking, an extension should be sought. If there are insufficient materials or an absence of the contextual information needed to understand the materials, the missing information should be requested from the colleague under review.

- The review should be based on standards. To prevent personal preference from prevailing, standards for effective teaching based on institutional, college, or departmental policies should be used in making judgments about teaching. Often, professional associations have documents that contain teaching standards as well. Peer reviewers should make sure that they obtain copies of these standards in advance of the review. If they are not available from any of these sources, a discussion of standards is necessary at the start of the review. They should be made explicit so that the basis for the review is articulated.

- Conclusions should be tied to evidence. Statements about the teaching of the colleague should be rooted in the specifics of the documentation that has been provided (e.g., a finding that the instructor lacks content knowledge should be supported by references to some particular mistakes or omissions that have surfaced in the review of materials or classroom performance).

- Summative peer review conducted at personnel decision-making checkpoints (promotion and tenure, contract extension, merit pay) should be comprehensive and comparative. Unlike formative peer review of teaching, summative review should focus on overall performance. While judgments about this performance should be grounded in specifics, the attempt should be to assess the teaching holistically over an extended period of time and range of conditions, rather than to focus on a given instance. For this purpose, then, isolated findings should not determine the conclusions so much as general patterns. These patterns need to be viewed within the context of the teaching performance of the colleague's peers as well. (Example: Is the involvement in teaching improvement efforts heavier, lighter, or about the same as the involvement of others in these activities within the department?   Should it be so, given the context of the department and expectations for the colleague?)

Peer review should be thoughtfully conducted. Reviewers should have the opportunity to engage in meaningful dialogue with other peers while the process takes place. A hallmark of an effective review is that the reviewers themselves learn through the process. As they surface teaching issues for judgment, their conversation should help to illuminate the issues involved. The review should culminate in a written summary that is thorough, grounded in evidence, and clear in its conclusions.

REFERENCES

Cohen, P., & McKeachie, W. (1980). The role of colleagues in the evaluation of college teaching. *Improving College and University Teaching, 28* (4) 147-154.

Chapter 4

Identifying the Focus of a Peer Review of Teaching System

Peer review systems should concentrate on those things that peers are most able to judge. Often, however, there is a second-order function of peer review: Peers are asked to review judgments and evidence submitted by others. For example, in a promotion consideration, peers will be looking at a dossier that contains multiple kinds of evidence from various sources, ranging from student ratings of instruction to self-assessment by the person being reviewed to colleagues' opinions of course syllabi. The peer can thus be involved at two stages: providing an initial commentary on some aspect of the teaching for either formative or summative purposes, or judging the accumulated evidence from multiple sources.

AREAS OF FOCUS

As has been indicated earlier, colleagues are generally considered the ideal reviewers for those aspects of teaching that involve subject matter expertise and pedagogical strategies specific to the discipline (effective ways to help students to understand and apply force field analysis, for example). Throughout the literature on peer review, experts enumerate its different areas of focus.

Seldin (1984, pp. 139-140) includes the following:

1. Selection and mastery of course content
2. Appropriateness of course objectives and instructional materials

3. Appropriate methodology for teaching specified sections of courses

4. Appropriate techniques to foster and measure student learning

5. Course organization

6. Student achievement based on exams, projects, presentations, and reports

7. Concern for and interest in teaching

8. Homework assignments, textbooks, and handouts

Cohen and McKeachie (1980) enumerate four broad areas for colleague assessment, including the second-order function mentioned above. The areas are elements of course design, instructional methods and materials, evaluation of students, and integration and interpretation of information gathered by others. Specific subtopics are included under each area:

1. Course goals/course content
   - Appropriateness of course goals
   - Coverage of basic course content
   - Currency of course content
   - Appropriateness of student work requirements

2. Instructional methods and materials
   - Suitability of methods of instruction to course goals
   - Appropriateness of reading list for the course
   - Reasonableness of time and efforts required to complete assignments
   - Appropriateness of handouts and learning aids
   - Suitability of media materials to course

3. Evaluation of students' work
   - Inclusion of higher order cognitive processes on exams and assignments
   - Reasonableness of length and difficulty of examinations
   - Degree of cognitive challenge of written assignments
   - Reasonableness of length and effort required to complete writing assignments
   - Appropriateness of grading criteria

4. Integration and interpretation
   • Interpretation of student ratings within the context of the course that is rated
   • Determination of criteria used for evaluation
   • Weighting of criteria used in determining teaching effectiveness

French-Lazovik's treatment of the issue of areas that peers should assess (1981, pp. 79-81) advocates asking the following questions:

1. What is the quality of materials used in teaching?
   • Are these materials current?
   • Do they represent the best work in the field?
   • Are they adequate and appropriate to course goals?
   • Do they represent superficial or thorough coverage of course materials?

2. What kind of intellectual tasks were set by the teacher for the students (or did the teacher succeed in getting students to set for themselves), and how did the students perform?
   • What was the level of intellectual performance achieved by the students?
   • What kinds of work was given an A? a B? a C?
   • Did the students learn what the department curriculum expected for this course?
   • How adequately do the tests or assignments represent the kinds of student performance specified in the course objectives?

3. How knowledgeable is this faculty member in the subjects taught?
   • Has the instructor kept in thoughtful contact with developments in his or her field?
   • Is there evidence of acquaintance with the ideas and findings of other scholars?

4. Has this faculty member assumed responsibilities related to the department's or university's teaching mission?
   - Has he or she become a departmental or college citizen in regard to teaching responsibilities?
   - Does this faculty member recognize problems that hinder good teaching, and does he or she take a responsible part in trying to solve them?
   - Is the involvement of the faculty member appropriate to his or her academic level?

5. To what extent is this faculty member trying to achieve excellence in teaching?
   - Has he or she sought feedback about teaching quality, explored alternative teaching methods, made changes to increase student learning?
   - Has he or she sought aid in trying new teaching ideas?
   - Has he or she developed special teaching materials or participated in cooperative efforts aimed at upgrading teaching quality?

EVIDENCE OF PERFORMANCE

Multiple types of evidence are available for making judgments on teaching performance questions. The reviewer is not limited to classroom observation. In enumerating the kinds of evidence that can be explored during peer reviews, French-Lazovik reveals the wide range of evidence that can be surveyed:

1. Course outlines
2. Syllabi
3. Reading lists
4. Texts, study guides, nonprint materials, and handouts
5. Problem sets, assignments
6. Copies of graded examinations, examples of graded research papers
7. Examples of teacher's feedback to students on written work
8. Grade distribution and descriptions of student performances
9. Examples of completed assignments
10. Records of service on department or institutional committees dealing with teaching issues (curriculum, honors program, etc.)

11. Descriptions of activities in supervising graduate students learning to teach

12. Evidence of the design of new courses

13. Statements of what activities the faculty member has engaged in to improve his or her teaching

14. Examples of questionnaires used for formative purposes

15. Examples of changes made on the basis of feedback

To these, Malik (1996) adds the reflective memo composed by the faculty member being reviewed. Quinlan (1996) talks about the course portfolio as a way of presenting many of these documents coherently.

Individual departments will choose to focus on some of these areas and types of evidence or on additional ones that they identify. In addition, other areas for review or types of evidence may be identified at the college or institutional levels. In Part II, the major areas and types of evidence are discussed and resources are provided for assessing each.

REFERENCES

Cohen, P., & McKeachie, W. (1980). The role of colleagues in the evaluation of college teaching. *Improving College and University Teaching, 28* (4), 147-154.

French-Lazovik, G. (1981). Peer review: Documentary evidence in the evaluation of teaching. In J. Millman (Ed.), *Handbook of Teacher Evaluation* (pp. 73-89). Thousand Oaks, CA: Sage.

Malik, D. (1996). Peer review of teaching: External review of course content. *Innovative Higher Education, 20,* 277-285.

Quinlan, K. (1996). Involving peers in the evaluation and improvement of teaching: A menu of strategies. *Innovative Higher Education, 20,* 299-307.

Seldin, P. (1984). *Changing practices in faculty evaluation.* San Francisco, CA: Jossey-Bass.

Part II
Resources and Forms

Chapter 5

Peer Review of Course Materials

Course materials are very important in supporting the learning that takes place in a course. They promote in-class learning and are also critical in shaping out-of-class experiences. Students with strong visual learning styles rely heavily on written course materials. The way in which an instructor uses print or digital materials and the content of the materials themselves provide a window on the course philosophy, expectations, scope, and presentation of subject matter. When it comes to assessing the accuracy and adequacy of instructional materials, peers are in an ideal position. Indeed, most writers on peer review see review of course materials as the optimal way in which peers can be involved.

Arguments for the review of course materials include the relative unobtrusiveness of the method: Classrooms do not have to be interrupted in order to do these reviews. Convenience is another factor: Reviews can take place at a time and place suitable to the schedule of the reviewer and do not require special preparations on the part of the teacher being reviewed. Third, the power of disclosure is often quite high: A look at a test can tell much about the level of learning goals in the course, the instructor's perception of what is important, and the instructor's pedagogical style toward the students. Graded tests, written work, or projects can tell all of the above, plus indicate how an instructor provides feedback to learners and implements an assessment scheme. Finally, reviewers can gain insights into their own teaching through working with sets of questions that enumerate characteristics of effective course materials. Good sets of questions are posed by Braskamp and Ory (1994, pp. 289-90), Keig and Waggoner (1994, pp. 61-62), and Nordstrom (1995, p. 131). Several sets of such questions are contained in the resource materials section of this chapter.

FOR FORMATIVE EVALUATION

For formative evaluation, use of course materials can enable a mentor or mentor team to see an instructor's philosophy enacted. Regular and thoughtful review of materials can alert mentors to the areas in which a given instructor excels and also to ways in which improvement can be cultivated. When used in peer dialogue groups, exchanges of materials, such as course syllabi, can promote reflective discussion about the overall goals of the academic unit, ways of effectively motivating and facilitating the success of the students, and the like. Ideas can be shared for the enrichment of all, cultivating teaching as "community property" and intellectual activity.

FOR SUMMATIVE EVALUATION

When used in summative evaluation, review of course materials is normally conducted to provide one point of information on the instructor's overall effectiveness, compared with others in the academic unit or profession. Often, this work is delegated to one or two peer reviewers, who then write an assessment that becomes part of the final dossier that is reviewed.

The voluminousness of course materials becomes an important issue and potential drawback to this approach. When a review is covering several years of work, whole file drawers of course materials could conceivably be at issue. Deciding how to choose representative syllabi, tests, course notes, handouts, computer software, or other materials can be done in several ways. The most frequent is to ask the faculty member being reviewed to submit a portfolio of materials. One would expect that in this case, the teacher would choose those things that are considered best for summative reviews or perhaps things that are problematic for formative reviews. Another method is to make specific requests, based on concerns within the department. For example, if a given course is the first in a sequence for which it is necessary that students build on skills of the prior course, requesting to see a copy of the final exam or course project requirement for that course might be an important way to see if the course is serving its function in the sequence. If the unit is working to cultivate student-centered teaching, the review team might choose to take a look at the course syllabus for a critical introductory course and review it according to principles of student-centered learning. For summative purposes, it is probably best for certain documents to be specified for review so that all instructors are treated similarly. Such requirements might specify, at minimum, the submission of the course syllabus for particular courses of interest (including bibliographies) and the final exam or project format for these courses.

MATERIALS FOR PEER REVIEW

Course materials that can be the focus of peer review include:

1. Materials that communicate course policy and practices:
   - Syllabus
   - Ground rules for discussion
   - Course guides
   - Teaching evaluation instruments

2. Materials that communicate content:
   - Course packets
   - Texts
   - Bibliographies
   - Overhead transparencies
   - Handouts
   - Computer simulations, videotapes, and other multimedia supplements

3. Materials that set assignments and assess student performance:
   - Tests
   - Project assignment directions and handouts
   - Classroom exercises (case studies, learning group tasks)

4. Instructor comments on student work:
   - Graded papers or tests
   - Journals, and email exchanges

OVERALL GUIDELINES

It is important to remember that course materials are not the course. Although they can be powerful indicators of an instructor's approach, there can also be a gap between what the instructor intends to do as expressed on paper and how these intentions are enacted. It is possible (although not too likely) that an instructor with clear and well-organized class handouts can be rude to students and rambling and inaccurate in class. Combining review of course materials with evidence gathered in other ways is necessary to arrive at a full picture.

Understanding the instructor's rationale and the context of the course is important in evaluating course materials. For formative review, instructors may provide this orally in informal discussions with the reviewer. In the case of summative review, this will generally be done in writing as part of the dossier.

Given the specialized nature of many course materials, the peer reviewer may be unfamiliar with the content of specific courses but may still be able to review their basic format, tone, and the appropriateness of the materials. It may be necessary to solicit the opinions of others in the field of specialization to review accuracy and currency of content.

Procedures for Formative Evaluation of Course Materials

1. Collect a representative sample (across courses and time) and information about the context in which they are used.
2. Prior to the review, identify the instructor's questions or concerns so that these can be addressed in your review.
3. Review the materials (instruments for helping to do this are in the resource materials section).
4. Within two weeks of conducting the review, schedule a feedback conversation with the instructor about the review. Constructive feedback techniques are described in Chapter 3.
5. Remain available for help as issues arise in the future.

Procedures for Summative Evaluation of Course Materials

1. Collect a representative (across courses and time) sample of materials and information about the context in which they are used.
2. Identify standards for these materials in the field of study or model materials prepared by others in the department.

3. Decide whether certain instruments are to be used and apply them consistently. (Instruments for helping to do this are in the resource materials section of this chapter.)

4. Review the materials.

5. Report on the results either by using a narrative approach or by submitting checklists or other ratings sheets.

Resource Materials:
Peer review of course materials

POLICIES PEER REVIEW FORMS
> The Syllabus: The Document Itself
> The Course Described by the Document
> Course Guidelines, Ground rules for Discussion, and
>   Other Policy and/or Procedure Documents
> Formative Teaching Evaluation Instruments for Student Feedback
> Summative Teaching Evaluation Instruments for Student Feedback

CONTENT PEER REVIEW FORMS
> Course Packet and Textbook Content
> Course Bibliographies
> Overhead Transparencies or Presentation Slides
> Course Handouts
> Multimedia Course Materials

ASSIGNMENTS PEER REVIEW FORMS
> Tests
> Class Assignments and Course Exercise Sheets

INSTRUCTOR COMMENTS PEER REVIEW FORM
> Instructor Comments on Student Work

PEER REVIEW OF THE SYLLABUS:
THE DOCUMENT ITSELF

For formative use: Focus on providing comments.
For summative use: Complete ratings and use comments to explain them.

	Exceeds level of expected qualities	Meets level on all qualities	Meets level on most qualities	Meets level on some qualities	Meets no/few expected qualities
Completeness	5	4	3	2	1

Does it have each of the
following, if relevant?

• Course information

• Instructor information

• Information on course readings

• Goals and objectives of course

• Policies on grading, academic
  misconduct, late work, absences,
  safety issues, accommodations for
  special needs

• Calendar of class activities

• Descriptions of assignments
  and dates due

• Support services available

Comment:

Chism, N.V.N. (1999). *Peer Review of Teaching: A Sourcebook.* Bolton, MA: Anker Publishing Co., Inc.

PEER REVIEW OF THE SYLLABUS:
THE DOCUMENT ITSELF (Continued)

	Exceeds level of expected qualities	Meets level on all qualities	Meets level on most qualities	Meets level on some qualities	Meets no/few expected qualities
Clarity of communication	5	4	3	2	1

- Is the syllabus clear?
- Are rights, responsibilities, and consequences spelled out?
- Is information internally consistent?
- Consistent with department or university policy?

Comment:

Appropriateness of tone	5	4	3	2	1

- Does the syllabus further rapport and respect between instructor and students?
- Does it communicate a helpful, positive attitude?
- Is it motivational, nonthreatening?
- Does it communicate the challenge of the course?

Comment:

Chism, N.V.N. (1999). *Peer Review of Teaching: A Sourcebook.* Bolton, MA: Anker Publishing Co., Inc.

PEER REVIEW OF THE SYLLABUS:
THE DOCUMENT ITSELF (Continued)

	Exceeds level of expected qualities	Meets level on all qualities	Meets level on most qualities	Meets level on some qualities	Meets no/few expected qualities
Professional appearance	5	4	3	2	1

- Is it formatted well?
- Are the grammar and spelling correct?
- Is it attractive?

Comment:

Other

Chism, N.V.N. (1999). *Peer Review of Teaching: A Sourcebook.* Bolton, MA: Anker Publishing Co., Inc.

PEER REVIEW OF THE SYLLABUS:
THE COURSE DESCRIBED BY THE DOCUMENT

For formative use: Focus on providing comments.
For summative use: Complete ratings and use comments to explain them.

Exceeds level of expected qualities	Meets level on all qualities	Meets level on most qualities	Meets level on some qualities	Meets no/few expected qualities

Currency of content

5   4   3   2   1

- Does this course portray the current state of the field in this area?

- Does it use readings that reflect the latest scholarship?

Comment:

Fit within the curriculum

5   4   3   2   1

- Does the course fulfill expectations of the academic unit for content and process skills needed for subsequent courses?

- Does it match the catalog description and expected overall fit within the curriculum of the institution?

- Does it duplicate other courses or is it undesirably idiosyncratic to one topic area or school of thinking?

Comment:

Chism, N.V.N. (1999). *Peer Review of Teaching: A Sourcebook.* Bolton, MA: Anker Publishing Co., Inc.

PEER REVIEW OF THE SYLLABUS:
THE COURSE DESCRIBED BY THE DOCUMENT (Continued)

	Exceeds level of expected qualities	Meets level on all qualities	Meets level on most qualities	Meets level on some qualities	Meets no/few expected qualities
Level of challenge	5	4	3	2	1

• Does the course require students to do an appropriate amount of reading and other assignments?

• Are these at an appropriate level of challenge?

Comment:

Pacing	5	4	3	2	1

• Is the course calendar realistic?
• Has the instructor selected a reasonable amount of content for the time allotted?

• Are the due dates for assignments distributed well?

Comment:

Chism, N.V.N. (1999). *Peer Review of Teaching: A Sourcebook.* Bolton, MA: Anker Publishing Co., Inc.

PEER REVIEW OF THE SYLLABUS:
THE COURSE DESCRIBED BY THE DOCUMENT (Continued)

	Exceeds level of expected qualities	Meets level on all qualities	Meets level on most qualities	Meets level on some qualities	Meets no/few expected qualities

Testing and grading

5   4   3   2   1

- Do the students receive frequent feedback?
- Are the grading policies fair and appropriate for the goals?

Comment:

Student-centeredness

5   4   3   2   1

- Do the office hours or other information portray that the instructor is accessible for help?
- Are other resources available to the student?
- Do the activities show a concern for active student engagement?

Comment:

Other

Chism, N.V.N. (1999). *Peer Review of Teaching: A Sourcebook.* Bolton, MA: Anker Publishing Co., Inc.

PEER REVIEW OF COURSE GUIDELINES, GROUND RULES FOR DISCUSSION, AND OTHER POLICY AND/OR PROCEDURE DOCUMENTS

For formative use: Focus on providing comments.
For summative use: Complete ratings and use comments to explain them.

	Exceeds level of expected qualities	Meets level on all qualities	Meets level on most qualities	Meets level on some qualities	Meets no/few expected qualities

Clarity of communication

5	4	3	2	1

- Is rationale clear?
- Are rights, responsibilities, and consequences spelled out?
- Is information internally consistent?
- Is it consistent with department or university policy?

Comment:

Appropriateness of tone

5	4	3	2	1

- Does the document further the rapport between instructor and students?
- Is it motivational, nonthreatening?

Comment:

Chism, N.V.N. (1999). *Peer Review of Teaching: A Sourcebook.* Bolton, MA: Anker Publishing Co., Inc.

PEER REVIEW OF COURSE GUIDELINES, GROUND RULES FOR DISCUSSION, AND OTHER POLICY AND/OR PROCEDURE DOCUMENTS (Continued)

	Exceeds level of expected qualities	Meets level on all qualities	Meets level on most qualities	Meets level on some qualities	Meets no/few expected qualities

Instructional value

5	4	3	2	1

- Is consistent with the goals and content of the course?
- Does it suggest helpful ways of achieving success?

Comment:

Professional appearance

5	4	3	2	1

- Is it formatted well?
- Are the grammar and spelling correct?

Comment:

Other

Chism, N.V.N. (1999). *Peer Review of Teaching: A Sourcebook.* Bolton, MA: Anker Publishing Co., Inc.

PEER REVIEW OF
FORMATIVE TEACHING EVALUATION INSTRUMENTS
FOR STUDENT FEEDBACK*

For formative use: Focus on providing comments.
For summative use: Complete ratings and use comments to explain them.

	Exceeds level of expected qualities	Meets level on all qualities	Meets level on most qualities	Meets level on some qualities	Meets no/few expected qualities

Allows students to provide detailed comments

• Has open-ended items and sufficient writing space.

| 5 | 4 | 3 | 2 | 1 |

Comment:

Is tailored to goals and practices of course

• Asks about specific activities, handouts, content coverage, etc.

| 5 | 4 | 3 | 2 | 1 |

Comment:

Asks students for recommendations for change

• Prompts students to think about specific issues such as textbook, laboratories, and what would work better.

| 5 | 4 | 3 | 2 | 1 |

Comment:

Chism, N.V.N. (1999). *Peer Review of Teaching: A Sourcebook.* Bolton, MA: Anker Publishing Co., Inc.

PEER REVIEW OF
FORMATIVE TEACHING EVALUATION INSTRUMENTS
FOR STUDENT FEEDBACK* (Continued)

	Exceeds level of expected qualities	Meets level on all qualities	Meets level on most qualities	Meets level on some qualities	Meets no/few expected qualities
Provides opportunities for unsolicited data • Asks: "Are there any other thoughts?"	5	4	3	2	1

Comment:

Other

(*Use to evaluate formative purpose instruments, those intended primarily for the instructor's own use at midcourse or at end of course for the purpose of suggesting changes for improvement.)

Chism, N.V.N. (1999). *Peer Review of Teaching: A Sourcebook.* Bolton, MA: Anker Publishing Co., Inc.

PEER REVIEW OF
SUMMATIVE TEACHING EVALUATION INSTRUMENTS
FOR STUDENT FEEDBACK*

For formative use: Focus on providing comments.
For summative use: Complete ratings and use comments to explain them.

Yes   No   Results can be summarized easily
                 (Uses numbers that can be averaged, text categories
                 that can be analyzed for patterns quickly)

Yes   No   Provides comparison data
                 (Expected norms or average scores of other
                 instructors using this instrument are available)

Yes   No   Is valid and reliable
                 (Focuses on what it intends to measure,
                 has history of consistent results)

Yes   No   Asks for global information
                 (Taps into broad dimensions of teaching,
                 rather than course-specific issues)

Yes   No   Is clear
                 (Provides explicit directions for students
                 and unambiguous items)

Overall evaluation form rating:

Satisfactory   Unsuitable for use

(*For summative purpose instruments, intended primarily for decision-making to provide comparative data in summative form.)

Chism, N.V.N. (1999). *Peer Review of Teaching: A Sourcebook.* Bolton, MA: Anker Publishing Co., Inc.

PEER REVIEW OF
COURSE PACKET AND TEXTBOOK CONTENT

For formative use: Focus on providing comments.
For summative use: Complete ratings and use comments to explain them.

	Excellent	Very Good	Good	Fair	Poor
Match with goals of course	5	4	3	2	1

Comment:

Accuracy of content	5	4	3	2	1

Comment:

Currency of content	5	4	3	2	1

Comment:

Multiple viewpoints presented	5	4	3	2	1

Comment:

Interest level	5	4	3	2	1

Comment:

Appropriateness of reading level	5	4	3	2	1

Comment:

Attractiveness	5	4	3	2	1

Comment:

Chism, N.V.N. (1999). *Peer Review of Teaching: A Sourcebook.* Bolton, MA: Anker Publishing Co., Inc.

PEER REVIEW OF
COURSE PACKET AND TEXTBOOK CONTENT (Continued)

	Excellent	Very Good	Good	Fair	Poor
Appropriateness of amount of reading	5	4	3	2	1

Comment:

Clarity of organization	5	4	3	2	1

Comment:

User friendliness	5	4	3	2	1

Comment:

Reputation and expertise of authors	5	4	3	2	1

Comment:

Fair use of copyright	5	4	3	2	1

Comment:

Other

(It is important that groups using this form define their standards for what each of the descriptors in this row mean within their context on each item.)

Chism, N.V.N. (1999). *Peer Review of Teaching: A Sourcebook.* Bolton, MA: Anker Publishing Co., Inc.

PEER REVIEW OF
COURSE BIBLIOGRAPHIES

For formative use: Focus on providing comments.
For summative use: Complete ratings and use comments to explain them.

	Excellent	Very Good	Good	Fair	Poor
Currency of works listed	5	4	3	2	1
Comment:					
Importance of works cited	5	4	3	2	1
Comment:					
Thoroughness of bibliography	5	4	3	2	1
Comment:					
Completeness of citations	5	4	3	2	1
Comment:					
If annotated, usefulness of summaries	5	4	3	2	1
Comment:					
Appropriateness for course	5	4	3	2	1
Comment:					

Chism, N.V.N. (1999). *Peer Review of Teaching: A Sourcebook.* Bolton, MA: Anker Publishing Co., Inc.

PEER REVIEW OF
COURSE BIBLIOGRAPHIES (Continued)

	Excellent	Very Good	Good	Fair	Poor
Appropriateness for level of student	5	4	3	2	1

Comment:

Relationship to course content	5	4	3	2	1

Comment:

Other

(It is important that groups using this form define their standards for what each of the descriptors in this row means within their context on each item.)

Chism, N.V.N. (1999). *Peer Review of Teaching: A Sourcebook.* Bolton, MA: Anker Publishing Co., Inc.

PEER REVIEW OF
OVERHEAD TRANSPARENCIES OR PRESENTATION SLIDES

For formative use: Focus on providing comments.
For summative use: Complete ratings and use comments to explain them.

	Excellent	Very Good	Good	Fair	Poor
Enhances representation of course content	5	4	3	2	1

Comment:

Expresses content clearly	5	4	3	2	1

Comment:

Presents material legibly	5	4	3	2	1

Comment:

Displays appropriate amounts of material	5	4	3	2	1

Comment:

Contains accurate content	5	4	3	2	1

Comment:

Shows evidence of proofreading	5	4	3	2	1

Comment:

Other

(It is important that groups using this form define their standards for what each of the descriptors in this row means within their context on each item.)

Chism, N.V.N. (1999). *Peer Review of Teaching: A Sourcebook.* Bolton, MA: Anker Publishing Co., Inc.

PEER REVIEW OF
COURSE HANDOUTS

For formative use: Focus on providing comments.
For summative peer review use: Complete ratings and use comments to explain them.

	Excellent	Very Good	Good	Fair	Poor
Supplements course content	5	4	3	2	1

Comment:

Contains accurate content	5	4	3	2	1

Comment:

Shows evidence of proofreading	5	4	3	2	1

Comment:

Is at appropriate reading level	5	4	3	2	1

Comment:

Is at adequate level of detail	5	4	3	2	1

Comment:

Demonstrates instructional skills	5	4	3	2	1

Comment:

Shows creativity (if applicable)	5	4	3	2	1

Comment:

Other

(It is important that groups using this form define their standards for what each of the descriptors in this row means within their context on each item.)

Chism, N.V.N. (1999). *Peer Review of Teaching: A Sourcebook.* Bolton, MA: Anker Publishing Co., Inc.

PEER REVIEW OF MULTIMEDIA COURSE MATERIALS

For formative use: Focus on providing comments.
For summative use: Complete ratings and use comments to explain them.

Overall Items

	Excellent	Very Good	Good	Fair	Poor
Match with goals of course	5	4	3	2	1

Comment:

Accuracy of content	5	4	3	2	1

Comment:

Currency of content	5	4	3	2	1

Comment:

Production quality	5	4	3	2	1

Comment:

Interest level	5	4	3	2	1

Comment:

Chism, N.V.N. (1999). *Peer Review of Teaching: A Sourcebook.* Bolton, MA: Anker Publishing Co., Inc.

PEER REVIEW OF
MULTIMEDIA COURSE MATERIALS (Continued)

	Excellent	Very Good	Good	Fair	Poor
Attractiveness	5	4	3	2	1
Comment:					
Appropriateness of length	5	4	3	2	1
Comment:					
Appropriate level of difficulty	5	4	3	2	1
Comment:					
Clarity of organization	5	4	3	2	1
Comment:					
User friendliness	5	4	3	2	1
Comment:					

Chism, N.V.N. (1999). *Peer Review of Teaching: A Sourcebook.* Bolton, MA: Anker Publishing Co., Inc.

PEER REVIEW OF
MULTIMEDIA COURSE MATERIALS (Continued)

Optional Items

	Excellent	Very Good	Good	Fair	Poor
Permits interactivity	5	4	3	2	1

Comment:

Permits self pacing	5	4	3	2	1

Comment:

Provides branching options	5	4	3	2	1

Comment:

Provides user feedback	5	4	3	2	1

Comment:

Provides accommodations for students with special needs	5	4	3	2	1

Comment:

Other

(It is important that groups using this form define their standards for what each of the descriptors in this row means within their context on each item.)

Chism, N.V.N. (1999). *Peer Review of Teaching: A Sourcebook.* Bolton, MA: Anker Publishing Co., Inc.

PEER REVIEW OF TESTS

For formative use: Focus on providing comments.
For summative use: Complete ratings and use comments to explain them.

	Excellent	Very Good	Good	Fair	Poor
Clarity of directions	5	4	3	2	1

Comment:

Match of content to course goals	5	4	3	2	1

Comment:

Legibility and layout	5	4	3	2	1

Comment:

Evidence of proofreading	5	4	3	2	1

Comment:

Appropriateness of length	5	4	3	2	1

Comment:

Clarity of items	5	4	3	2	1

Comment:

Appropriate level of challenge	5	4	3	2	1

Comment:

Chism, N.V.N. (1999). *Peer Review of Teaching: A Sourcebook.* Bolton, MA: Anker Publishing Co., Inc.

PEER REVIEW OF TESTS (Continued)

	Excellent	Very Good	Good	Fair	Poor
Inclusion of higher order thinking	5	4	3	2	1

Comment:

Organization of content	5	4	3	2	1

Comment:

Other

(It is important that groups using this form define their standards for what each of the descriptors in this row means within their context on each item.)

Chism, N.V.N. (1999). *Peer Review of Teaching: A Sourcebook.* Bolton, MA: Anker Publishing Co., Inc.

PEER REVIEW OF CLASS ASSIGNMENTS
AND COURSE EXERCISE SHEETS

For formative use: Focus on providing comments.
For summative use: Complete ratings and use comments to explain them.

	Excellent	Very Good	Good	Fair	Poor
Supplements course content	5	4	3	2	1

Comment:

Provides clear directions	5	4	3	2	1

Comment:

Encourages meaningful learning experiences	5	4	3	2	1

Comment:

Is at appropriate level of challenge	5	4	3	2	1

Comment:

Outlines assessment method	5	4	3	2	1

Comment:

Clearly states purpose	5	4	3	2	1

Comment:

PEER REVIEW OF CLASS ASSIGNMENTS
AND COURSE EXERCISE SHEETS (Continued)

	Excellent	Very Good	Good	Fair	Poor
Demonstrates instructor creativity	5	4	3	2	1

Comment:

	Excellent	Very Good	Good	Fair	Poor
Promotes student engagement	5	4	3	2	1

Comment:

	Excellent	Very Good	Good	Fair	Poor
Provides adequate time and resources for completion	5	4	3	2	1

Comment:

Other

(It is important that groups using this form define their standards for what each of the descriptors in this row means within their context on each item.)

Chism, N.V.N. (1999). *Peer Review of Teaching: A Sourcebook.* Bolton, MA: Anker Publishing Co., Inc.

PEER REVIEW OF
INSTRUCTOR COMMENTS ON STUDENT WORK

For formative use: Focus on providing comments.
For summative use: Complete ratings and use comments to explain them.

	Excellent	Very Good	Good	Fair	Poor
Feedback is clear	5	4	3	2	1
Comment:					
Feedback is legible	5	4	3	2	1
Comment:					
Feedback is supportive of student efforts	5	4	3	2	1
Comment:					
Constructive suggestions are provided	5	4	3	2	1
Comment:					
Comments show consistency	5	4	3	2	1
Comment:					
Comments are motivational toward further progress	5	4	3	2	1
Comment:					

Chism, N.V.N. (1999). *Peer Review of Teaching: A Sourcebook.* Bolton, MA: Anker Publishing Co., Inc.

PEER REVIEW OF
INSTRUCTOR COMMENTS ON STUDENT WORK (Continued)

	Excellent	Very Good	Good	Fair	Poor
Comments show appropriate expectations for level of student	5	4	3	2	1

Comment:

Comments display content accuracy	5	4	3	2	1

Comment:

Amount of feedback is appropriate	5	4	3	2	1

Comment:

Other

(It is important that groups using this form define their standards for what each of the descriptors in this row means within their context on each item.)

Chism, N.V.N. (1999). *Peer Review of Teaching: A Sourcebook.* Bolton, MA: Anker Publishing Co., Inc.

REFERENCES

Braskamp, L., & Ory, J. (1994). *Assessing faculty work: Enhancing individual and institutional performance.* San Francisco, CA: Jossey-Bass.

Keig, L., & Waggoner, M. (1994). Collaborative peer review: The role of faculty in improving college teaching. *ASHE-ERIC Higher Education Report,* No. 2. Washington, DC: The George Washington University, Graduate School of Education and Human Development.

Nordstrom, K. (1995). Multiple-purpose use of a peer review of course instruction program in a multidisciplinary university department. *Journal on Excellence in College Teaching, 6* (3), 125-144.

Chapter 6

Classroom Observation

Classroom observation is perhaps the most familiar form of peer review. Unfortunately, it is the most prone to reliability problems, often the result when uninformed peers make brief visits and report from the perspective of their own biases. The evaluation literature makes it clear that the consistent presence of students in the classrooms makes them a better source of information about such things as an instructor's approach, fairness, clarity of explanations, and the like. Students, however, cannot be expected to be accurate judges of such areas as the subject matter competency of the instructor or the instructor's use of teaching strategies current to the discipline. For these purposes, peer review is important. The peer's experiential base and credibility with the instructor are also assets for this form of evaluation. Some insight on these aspects of teaching can be obtained through classroom observation. With proper understanding of how to observe classes, peers can use this method to provide data points for improvement and decision-making.

An advantage of classroom observation by peers is that the peer's own development may be fostered through the ideas obtained from watching a colleague. Reciprocal classroom observations are a strategy employed in many faculty development programs, such as the New Jersey Master Teacher Program (Golin, 1990). An interesting account of peer classroom observation is provided by Peter Elbow in the essay "One-to-One Faculty Development" (1980). In some cases, peer classroom observation is complemented by other methods, such as student interviewing or dialogue groups, for the purposes of mutual faculty development.

OVERALL GUIDELINES

1) It cannot be assumed that peer reviewers are skilled classroom observers. Academic units using peer classroom observation should engage potential reviewers in activities designed to explore observational goals and methods. They can watch videotapes together to generate ideas on what is important to look for, they can read and react to each other's narrative reports of the same videotaped class, they can use and compare ratings on a departmental rating form for classroom observation. A teaching consultant can lead training on classroom observation, suggesting and offering practice in various ways of approaching this task. Efforts on preparing faculty to do classroom observations increase reliability of the results.

2) A single classroom observation by one rater is not a reliable indicator of teaching quality. Lewis (1988), for example, recommends that classroom observations should be conducted at least three times to establish reliability for summative evaluation purposes; Muchinsky (1995) recommends that two reviewers must observe at least twice during the offering of a course. The viewpoints of multiple raters should be presented when possible.

3) Preobservation information is necessary to provide contextual information about the course, instructor, and students. It is best to obtain this face to face, but a telephone conversation or written description from the course instructor can be used if there are no opportunities for a meeting. Information that might be obtained is listed in the resource materials section for this chapter.

4) During the classroom observation, a variety of approaches can be used to focus the observation. These include a holistic approach followed by a narrative report, an analytical approach that uses a checklist or rating form to assess specific aspects of the class, videotaping, or more specialized systems such as teacher behavior coding instruments or mapping techniques.

5) The observer should try to be as unobtrusive as possible. The instructor might refer to the presence of the observer at the beginning of class if this seems necessary but should refrain from making explanatory comments that might affect the behavior of the students. If the reviewer is not staying for the whole class, the instructor should know this in advance.

6) To allow the instructor and class to relax into typical patterns of behavior, observing over a substantial amount of time is necessary. In the case of a one-hour class, the entire class should be observed. For longer classes, a one-hour segment can be chosen, based on the information gathered during the preobservation stage as to which segment would be most appropriate.

7) Following the observation, the observer should complete the notes, forms, or other reports while the information is fresh.

Procedures for Class Observation in the Formative Evaluation of Classroom Teaching

1) During the preobservation conference, information on the instructor's concerns and results of prior feedback should help focus the evaluation. The instructor, may, for example, ask the observer to pay particular attention to discussion-leading skills.

2) The approach used by the observer should permit the gathering of specific information so that concrete details and suggestions can be recorded for later review with the instructor. Extensive notes should be taken since a rich, descriptive record will be helpful in debriefing.

3) Personal feedback after the observation is essential. The peer and instructor should debrief the class session, with each providing reflections. The observer should provide constructive feedback with the goal of helping the instructor to map a strategy for improvement.

4) The observer should be available for follow-up observations or conversations with the instructor as the improvement plan is implemented.

Keig and Waggoner (1994, p. 95), summarizing the characteristics of effective programs of collaborative peer observation in place at several institutions, list other recommendations for using classroom observation in formative evaluation of teaching:

- Programs should be built on the premise [of improvement] . . . and should not be considered remedial.
- Faculty participation should be voluntary.
- The observed teacher and the observer should be trusted and respected by each other.
- Classroom visits should be reciprocal (a faculty member should be, in turn, observed and observer). . . .
- Observations should occur by invitation only (there should be no surprise visits).
- Participants should determine in advance what other procedures, if any, are to be employed in assessing teaching performance.
- Participants should also determine in advance what other procedures, if any, are to be employed in assessing performance.
- The lines of communication between the observed faculty member and the observer should be open (feedback should be both candid and tactful).
- A balance between praise and constructive criticism should guide the feedback process.
- Results should be kept strictly confidential and apart from the summative evaluation.

Procedures for Classroom Observation for the Summative Evaluation of Classroom Teaching

1) When information from a classroom observation is to be used summatively, particular care should be taken to assure the reliability of the observation.

Guidelines for how the observer should be chosen, how many observations should occur, how long the observations last, and what approach is used to gather and report data should be agreed upon in the department and followed consistently.

2) A set of criteria that the department determines to be characteristic of good classroom teaching should be developed and used to focus classroom observations.

3) The approach used by the observer should permit the gathering of information that is representative of the instructor's overall teaching and reported in a format that enables it to be compared with information from other instructors.

4) The report should provide information on the process used to gather feedback and the context in which the observations took place.

Useful advice for observing classroom teaching is provided in several guides including Millis (1992) and Sorcinelli (1984). Various checklists and ratings forms have been developed to assist peers with classroom observation. In general, they are based on characteristics of effective teaching that have been consistently identified in the literature, such as teacher organization, content knowledge, enthusiasm, rapport with students, and clarity. These methods include:

- Taking field notes
- Completing ratings forms
- Using teacher behavioral assessment systems

Samples of instruments and reporting formats are contained in the following resource materials section.

Resource Materials:
Classroom observation

PREPARATION FOR OBSERVATION
Preobservation Conference Form

THE NARRATIVE LOG

CLASSROOM OBSERVATION RATING FORMS
Template: Classroom Observation Rating Form
Narrative Prompt Forms
Checklist Forms
Scaled Rating Forms
Expanded CIAS Categories
Typical CIAS Category Sequences and Their Explanations

PREPARATION FOR OBSERVATION

In order for the peer reviewer to situate a classroom observation within the context of the total course and the instructor's development, a conference should be scheduled. Sometimes, this may be an extended discussion, while at other times, a note or telephone conversation may have to suffice. The following form provides examples of the kinds of information that might be sought from the instructor before a classroom observation takes place.

PREOBSERVATION CONFERENCE FORM

Prior to the scheduled observation, the peer reviewer might use the following form (or an adaptation of the form) to structure the discussion of the teaching context with the instructor to be reviewed. Information can focus on class goals, students, learning activities, and particular teaching style. The peer reviewer should request that the instructor bring a copy of the syllabus, text, and any pertinent material to help the reviewer understand the content and cognitive level of the course.

Instructor: .... Date: .... Time: ....

Course Number: .... Course Title: ....

Course Meeting Time: .... Level of Students: ....

1) What are the goals for the class that I will observe?

2) What are your plans for achieving these goals?

3) What teaching/learning activities will take place?

4) What have students been asked to do in preparation for this class?

5) Will this class be typical of your teaching style? If not, why?

6) (For formative review) What would you like me to focus on during the observation?

7) Are there other things that I should be aware of prior to the observation?

THE NARRATIVE LOG

The narrative log, used mainly for formative purposes, should describe verbal and nonverbal behavior, emphasizing what the reviewer sees rather than the reviewer's judgment. (Some reviewers use a double-entry format that lists descriptive material on the right of the page and reflections on the left.) It is particularly useful to record times when a behavior or activity occurred so that the structure of the class can be placed into context and the amount of time spent on certain activities can be assessed.

Narrative logs are used to help instructors review a class after it has occurred. They can stimulate recall and freeze the class in time for the purpose of examination. During a post-observation conference, the log can be used to trigger the instructor's consideration of fit of actions to goals, student learning issues, alternate ways that situations could have been handled, and the like. A much more convenient way of capturing such information is to use videotape; however, the presence of a camera in the classroom can cause nervousness on the parts of both the instructor and students, at least at first. Ways to use videotape effectively are summarized by Keig and Waggoner (1994).

Some topics that can focus the narrative log include:
- What is the instructor speaking about?
- What specific comments are being made?
- What types of questions are being asked?
- How are classroom learning activities organized?
  (Create a chart if necessary)
- What is the level of student interaction?
- What teaching strategies are being used?
- What are your impressions of what is being observed?
  (Kept separate from the observation)

Example of a Portion of a Double-Entry Narrative Log

Organized start, good student rapport

1:21 Dr. Smith arrives early and sets out materials to be used, aligns the overhead projector and tests it, and begins to greet students as they arrive. Three students talk with her during this time, two apparently asking for clarification of an assignment and one sharing an article with her. She reacts with great enthusiasm and surprise, conversing with the student about possible mutual acquaintances and experiences. At the bell time, all but three students are present and seated.

Nice atmosphere. Clear about goals for class. Appreciates students' contributions but is good at displacing off-topic statement. Only male students participate at this time. Evidence that students have read prior to class. Too much time spent setting up class? Class combines student and instructor choice of direction.

1:30 Dr. Smith begins with a joke about something in the morning's news. She then reviews what had happened in the last class and states the objectives of this class, which she phrases as: to be able to use learning style research in classroom instruction. She asks the students if they would like to state their special interests in this topic, based on their advanced reading. The first student to respond says that he is skeptical about the ability of Myers-Briggs instruments to accurately describe people. Dr. Smith does not respond directly, but writes on the board, "Accuracy of instruments" as a topic to be dealt with later. The next student feeds off the previous student's comment about the Myers-Briggs, talking about a job interview when it was used. Dr. Smith refocuses the topic by repeating, "What things would you like to talk about today with respect to classroom use?" Several students list ideas, which Smith summarizes and posts as "variety of things being assessed by learning style theorists," "match between instructional style and learning style," and "association of learning style and cultural background." Smith says that the discussion will be structured around these topics as well as four that she adds. This process has consumed seven minutes of class time.

CLASSROOM OBSERVATION RATING FORMS

A variety of preconstructed forms are available for the rating of classroom instruction by peer observers. These range from checklists of behaviors to higher inference forms that ask for the observer's assessment of the quality of the teaching. Some instruments are general in nature and are intended for use in a traditional classroom setting where lecture-discussion is the format. Other instruments are tailored to specific settings, such as the studio or laboratory or to specific learning formats, such as collaborative learning. Since it is important that the rating form match the context of the teaching, this resource materials section will illustrate general formats for forms and will present a list of items that can be used in putting together a form for the setting in which it will be used.

Format Considerations

Each form should contain course information, directions for completing the form, and items to be completed.

Course information. The form should contain specific information about the course and observation. For example, see template that follows.

Directions. The form should contain directions for reviewers. For example, see template that follows.

TEMPLATE: CLASSROOM OBSERVATION RATING FORM

Instructor: . . . . Date: . . . .

Time: . . . . Course Number: . . . .

Course Title: . . . . Course Meeting Time: . . . .

Level of Students: . . . . Number of Students Present: . . . .

Reviewer: . . . .

Directions: For formative use: Focus on providing comments.
For summative use: Complete ratings and use comments to explain them.
Ratings are on a scale of 5 = Extremely effective; 4 = Effective; 3 = Somewhat effective;
2 = Inconsistently effective; and 1 = Not at all effective.

Item Formats

The items that the rater will use are listed next. These may be in the following formats:

- Narrative prompt forms
- Checklist with or without comments
- Scaled rating form with or without comments

Chism, N.V.N. (1999). *Peer Review of Teaching: A Sourcebook.* Bolton, MA: Anker Publishing Co., Inc.

NARRATIVE PROMPT FORMS

Narrative prompt forms focus on prespecified target areas and call for extended comment incorporating the combined description and judgment of the reviewer. For example,

> *Teacher organization.* Comment on the extent to which the teacher made the class plan explicit, followed the plan, had the materials needed for the class, showed evidence of having prepared the content, and the like.

Examples of prompts in specific areas of instruction.

- *Variety and pacing of instruction.* Comment on the extent to which the teacher employed a variety of instructional strategies and paced the class for interest and accomplishment of the goals.
- *Content knowledge.* Comment on the importance, currency, and accuracy of the content presented by the instructor.
- *Presentation skills.* Comment on the instructor's voice, tone, fluency, eye contact, rate of speech, gestures, use of space.
- *Teacher-student rapport.* Comment on the verbal interaction present in class, the extent to which the teacher welcomed and appreciated student discussion, the teacher's openness to class suggestions and interpersonal skills.
- *Clarity.* Comment on the extent to which the teacher used examples, is clear with explanations or answers to student questions, defines new terms or concepts.

Examples of general prompts.

- What things went well for this instructor and/or the class?
- What things did not go so well during this particular class?
- What specific suggestions for improvement do you have?
- What things did you learn in the pre- or post-observation conference that influenced your observation and feedback?
- How does this instructor compare with others in the department?

Chism, N.V.N. (1999). *Peer Review of Teaching: A Sourcebook.* Bolton, MA: Anker Publishing Co., Inc.

CHECKLIST FORMS

Checklist forms, with or without space for comments, focus on description (the presence or absence of certain characteristics) and emphasize low-inference items. Items are chosen in accordance with the instructional values of the instructor's unit. The measures can be simply "yes" or "no" or can be measures of frequency, such as "Always, Often, Sometimes, Never." Comments can be used by the reviewer to explain the rationale for choosing the rating or for providing additional information. For example,

The instructor states the objectives of the class.   **Yes**   **No**

Comment:

Possible items for checklist forms (lower inference items).

Instructor organization
- The instructor arrives to class on time.
- The instructor states the relation of the class to the previous one.
- The instructor locates class materials as they are needed.
- The instructor knows how to use the educational technology needed for the class.
- The instructor posts class goals or objectives on the board or overhead.
- The instructor posts or verbally provides an outline of the organization of the class.
- The instructor makes transitional statements between class segments.
- The instructor follows the preset structure.
- The instructor conveys the purpose of each class activity.
- The instructor summarizes periodically and at the end of class.

Variety and pacing of instruction
- More than one form of instruction is used.
- During discussion, the instructor pauses after asking questions.
- The instructor accepts student responses.
- The instructor draws nonparticipating students into the discussion.
- The instructor prevents specific students from dominating the discussion.

Chism, N.V.N. (1999). *Peer Review of Teaching: A Sourcebook.* Bolton, MA: Anker Publishing Co., Inc.

- The instructor helps students extend their responses.
- The instructor maps the direction of the discussion.
- The instructor mediates conflict or differences of opinion.
- The instructor demonstrates active listening techniques.
- The instructor provides explicit directions for active learning tasks.
- The instructor allows enough time to complete active learning tasks, such as group work.
- The instructor specifies how active learning tasks will be evaluated.
- The instructor was able to complete the topics scheduled for the class.
- The instructor provides time for students to practice.

Content knowledge

- The instructor's statements are accurate according to the standards of the field.
- The instructor incorporates current research in the field.
- The instructor identifies sources, perspectives, and authorities in the field.
- The instructor communicates the reasoning process behind operations or concepts.

Presentation skills

- The instructor's voice is audible.
- The instructor varies the tone and pitch of voice for emphasis and interest.
- The instructor avoids distracting mannerisms.
- The instructor maintains eye contact throughout the class.
- The instructor avoids extended reading from notes or texts.
- The instructor spoke at a pace that allowed students to take notes.

Rapport with students

- The instructor addresses students by name.
- The instructor attends to student comprehension or puzzlement.
- The instructor provides feedback at given intervals.
- The instructor uses positive reinforcement.
- The instructor incorporates student ideas into the class.

Chism, N.V.N. (1999). *Peer Review of Teaching: A Sourcebook.* Bolton, MA: Anker Publishing Co., Inc.

Clarity

- The instructor defines new terms or concepts.
- The instructor elaborates or repeats complex information.
- The instructor uses examples to explain content.
- The instructor makes explicit statements drawing student attention to certain ideas.
- The instructor pauses during explanations to allow students to ask questions.

Chism, N.V.N. (1999). *Peer Review of Teaching: A Sourcebook.* Bolton, MA: Anker Publishing Co., Inc.

SCALED RATING FORMS

Rating forms with scales and with or without space for comments focus on higher inference evaluation of specific behaviors. Usually a 5-point scale with specific anchor words such as "Strongly Agree-Strongly Disagree, Effective-Ineffective, Excellent-Poor" is used. Arreola (1995) cautions that standards of performance be identified (e.g., "The syllabus contains the following items:" etc.) so that reviewers are rating the same thing, and labels on the rating scale are related to the criteria to be evaluated. He also says that interior points of the rating scale be labeled as well as end points. Others would argue that such precision is cumbersome and ignores the contextual differences between settings. For example, one department might expect a bibliography to be an essential part of a good syllabus, whereas less print-oriented departments might not. Within a given context, however, it is important that reviewers have some common understanding of what constitutes "excellent" as opposed to "very good," "fair," and the like.

Comments can go below each item, in spaces to the right or left of the item, or at the end of the form. When one form is used for a variety of situations, the rating N/A is provided in case certain specific behaviors may not applicable to the setting that is being observed. Illustration:

The instructor is well-prepared for class.	Extremely 5	Very well 4	Adequately 3	Inconsistently 2	Not at all 1 N/A	Comment

Sometimes, such instruments give behavioral indicators of general characteristics in order to increase the likelihood that raters will be attending to the same characteristics. In the above item, for example, the following might be included:

	Exceeds level of expected qualities	Meets level on all qualities	Meets level on most qualities	Meets level on some qualities	Meets no/few expected qualities
The instructor is well-prepared for class. (Arrives and starts promptly, has all materials ready and in order, has an articulated class plan, shows content preparation.)	5	4	3	2	1

Possible items for scaled ratings forms (higher inference items involving values).

Teacher organization

- The instructor is well-prepared for class.
- The objectives of the class are clearly stated.
- The instructor uses class time efficiently.
- The learning activities are well organized.
- The class remains focused on its objectives.

Instructional strategies

- The instructor's choice of teaching techniques is appropriate for the goals.
- The instructor has good questioning skills.
- The instructor raises stimulating and challenging questions.
- The instructor mediates discussion well.
- The class schedule proceeds at an appropriate pace.
- The instructor uses multimedia effectively.
- Board work is legible and organized.
- Course handouts are used effectively.
- The instructor provides clear directions for group work or other forms of active learning.
- The instructor facilitates group work well.
- The instructor helps students to learn from each other.
- The instructor helps students apply theory to solve problems.
- The instructor effectively holds class attention.
- The instructor provides an effective range of challenges.

Instruction in laboratories, studios, or field settings

- Experiments/exercises are well chosen and well organized.
- Procedures/techniques are clearly explained/demonstrated.
- The instructor is thoroughly familiar with experiments/exercises.
- The instructor is thoroughly familiar with equipment/tools used.
- Assistance is always available during experiments/exercises.

Chism, N.V.N. (1999). *Peer Review of Teaching: A Sourcebook.* Bolton, MA: Anker Publishing Co., Inc.

- Experiments/exercises are important supplements to course.
- Experiments/exercises develop important skills.
- Experiments/exercises are of appropriate length.
- Experiments/exercises are of appropriate level of difficulty.
- Experiments/exercises help to develop confidence in subject area.
- The instructor provides aid with interpretation of data.
- The instructor's emphasis on safety is evident.
- Criticism of procedures/techniques is constructive.
- The instructor works well with students and other parties in the setting.
- Clinical or field experiences are realistic.

Content knowledge
- The instructor is knowledgeable about the subject matter.
- The instructor is confident in explaining the subject matter.
- The instructor pitches instruction to an appropriate level.
- The instructor uses a variety of illustrations to explain content.
- The instructor provides for sufficient content detail.
- The instructor focuses on important content in the field.
- The instructor demonstrates intellectual curiosity toward new ideas or perspectives.
- The instructor incorporates views of women and minorities.
- The instructor corrects racist or sexist bias in assigned materials.

Presentation skills
- The instructor is an effective speaker.
- The instructor employs an appropriate rate of speech.
- The instructor uses classroom space well.
- The instructor is enthusiastic about the subject matter.
- The instructor makes the subject matter interesting.
- The instructor's command of English is adequate.

Chism, N.V.N. (1999). *Peer Review of Teaching: A Sourcebook.* Bolton, MA: Anker Publishing Co., Inc.

Rapport with students
- The instructor welcomes student participation.
- The instructor models good listening habits.
- The instructor motivates students.
- The instructor stimulates interest in the course subject(s).
- The instructor responds well to student differences.
- The instructor demonstrates a sense of humor.
- The instructor uses effective classroom management techniques.
- The instructor demonstrates flexibility in responding to student concerns or interests.
- The instructor welcomes multiple perspectives.
- The instructor anticipates student problems.
- The instructor treats students impartially.
- The instructor respects constructive criticism.
- The instructor does not express sexist or racist attitudes.
- The instructor is able to help many kinds of students.
- The instructor is sensitive to individual interests and abilities.

Clarity
- The instructor responds to questions clearly.
- The instructor emphasizes major points in the delivery of the subject matter.
- The instructor explains the subject matter clearly.
- The instructor relates course material to practical situations.

Chism, N.V.N. (1999). *Peer Review of Teaching: A Sourcebook.* Bolton, MA: Anker Publishing Co., Inc.

Impact on learning
- The instructor helps develop rational thinking.
- The instructor helps develop problem-solving ability.
- The instructor helps develop skills/techniques/views needed in field.
- The instructor broadens student views.
- The instructor encourages the development of students' analytic ability.
- The instructor provides a healthy challenge to former attitudes.
- The instructor helps develop students' creative capacity.
- The instructor fosters respect for diverse points of view.
- The instructor sensitizes students to views or feelings of others.
- The instructor helps develop students' decision-making abilities.
- The instructor develops students' appreciation of intellectual activity.
- The instructor develops students' cultural awareness.
- The instructor helps students develop awareness of the process used to gain new knowledge.
- The instructor stimulates independent thinking.

Overall
- The overall teaching ability of the instructor is high.

Chism, N.V.N. (1999). *Peer Review of Teaching: A Sourcebook.* Bolton, MA: Anker Publishing Co., Inc.

TEACHER BEHAVIOR SYSTEMS

Systematic processes for coding teacher behaviors have been developed by several researchers. Among the most popular is the Flanders Interaction Analysis System. It focuses on teacher talk and student talk and includes a category for other behaviors. Many other systems are modifications of the Flanders System and include nonverbal behaviors as well. The systems are used to provide precise analysis of classrooms and are especially suitable for situations in which the amount or kind of teacher talk is the main interest.

In one system, called the Cognitive Interaction Analysis System (CIAS), after a period of observing the class without recording, the rater makes a category notation every three seconds about the nature of the interaction that has occurred during that time period. Categories and a sample completed rating form follow for the Cognitive Interaction Analysis System, described in Lewis (1988).

EXPANDED CIAS CATEGORIES

1) Accepting student attitudes

      1 h Use of humor

      1 f Affective instructor comments

2) Positive reinforcement

3) Repeating a student response

      3 f Giving corrective feedback

      3 b Building on a student response

4) Asking questions

      4 c Knowledge/comprehension level

      4 e Application (example) level

      4 a Analysis level

      4 y Synthesis level

      4 j Evaluation (judgment) level

      4 f Affective questions

4s   Process or structure questions

4r   Rhetorical questions

4p   Probing questions

5) Lecturing

5v   Simultaneous visual and verbal presentation

5e   Using examples/analogies

5r   Reviewing

5x   Answering a student question

5m   Mumbling

5t   Reading verbatim from text/overhead/board/slide

6) Providing cues

6m   Focusing on main points

6d   Giving directions

6c   Calling on a student

6s   Giving assignments/process

6v   Cues with visual presentation

7) Criticism of student answer/behavior

8) Cognitive student talk

8c-8j   Answers to teacher questions

8n   Student doesn't know answer

8q   Student question

8h   Student laughter

8g   Students working in groups

8 i   Students working individually

9) Noncognitive student talk

0) Silence

0b   Writing on board/overhead without talking

0m   Mumbling (a general low roar)

0 l   Listening/watching

Some Typical CIAS Category Sequences and Their Explanations

Each sequence of CIAS codes is read from the top of the column to the bottom. The comment section interprets the interaction pattern which is represented by the codes to the left of it.

Sequence	Comment
6s 6s 6d 6d 6 6c 8q	This sequence indicates that the instructor began by giving the students an assignment (6s) or indicated a procedure which they should follow in completing an assignment. Directions for completing this process were then given (6d). The instructor then told the students what they were going to be covering that day in the lecture (6). This is followed by the instructor calling on a student (6c) who then asks a question (8q).
4a 4a 0 0 8a	In this sequence, the instructor asks a question which would be classified as being at the analysis level (4a). The question is then followed by six seconds of silence, or "think time" (0), and finally, the question is answered by a student (8a).

8q 8q 5x 5x	When the students ask a question, it is recorded as 8q. The instructor's answer to that question is recorded as 5x. This provides information as to whether the instructor is spending adequate time or too much time in answering each student's question.
4e 4e 8e 8e 8e 2 3 3b	This sequence shows that the instructor asked a question at the application level (4e), and it was answered by a student (8e). It took the student nine seconds to answer the question. This is typical for a higher-level question. The instructor then praised the student's answer (that is, "That's right, Joe."), repeated the student's answer so the rest of the class could hear it, and then used the student's answer to explain the concept further (3b).

REFERENCES

Arreola, R. (1995). *Developing a comprehensive faculty evaluation system: A handbook for college faculty and administrators on designing and operating a comprehensive faculty evaluation system.* Bolton, MA: Anker.

Elbow, P. (1980). One-to-one faculty development. In J. Noonan (Ed.), *Learning about teaching.* New Directions for Teaching and Learning, No. 4. San Francisco, CA: Jossey-Bass.

Golin, S. (1990). Four arguments for peer collaboration and student interviewing: The master faculty program. *AAHE Bulletin, 3* (4), 9-10.

Keig, L., & Waggoner, M. (1994). *Collaborative peer review: The role of faculty in improving college teaching.* ASHE-ERIC Higher Education Report, No. 2. Washington, DC: The George Washington University, Graduate School of Education and Human Development.

Lewis, K. (1988). Using an objective observation system to diagnose teaching problems. In K. Lewis & J. Lunde (Eds.), *Face to face* (pp. 137-157). Stillwater, OK: New Forums Press.

Millis, B. (1992) Conducting effective peer classroom observations. In D. Wulff and J. Nyquist (Eds.), *To Improve the Academy, 11* (pp. 189-206). Stillwater, OK: New Forums Press.

Muchinsky, P. (1995). Peer review of teaching: Lessons learned from military and industrial research on peer assessment. *Journal on Excellence in College Teaching, 6* (3), 17-30.

Sorcinelli, M. (1984). An approach to colleague evaluation of classroom instruction. *Journal of Instructional Development, 7* (4), 11-17.

Chapter 7

Leadership for Teaching:
Contributions to Scholarship of Teaching and Departmental Teaching Efforts

While the goal of much peer review is to improve and reward good classroom teaching, there is more to excellent teaching. This chapter focuses on leadership for teaching, both within the department, discipline, and across disciplines. In particular, it looks at the scholarship of teaching and contributions to departmental teaching efforts. In a sense, these activities can be considered research or service, and the extent to which this is true will depend somewhat on the institutional context and how such activities are defined. However, there is a sense in which these activities are organic to teaching, testifying to the depth of commitment, creativity, and student focus that teachers bring to their work.

SCHOLARSHIP OF TEACHING

One of the four types of scholarship discussed in Ernest Boyer's *Scholarship Reconsidered* (1990) is the scholarship of teaching. By this, Boyer means activities through which faculty explore conceptions central to the teaching of their field, assess the effects of different teaching strategies on student learning in the discipline, and pose new directions for exploration. These activities are demonstrated in the daily work of teaching. Teachers' use of classroom assessment techniques (Angelo & Cross, 1993) help them to explore systematically what prior knowledge and skills their students are bringing to the classroom, what they are learning, and how their students are attending to instructional interventions. Engaging in informal or formal classroom research projects is a sign that teachers take an interest in student learning and their own professional development. Peer reviewers working formatively can use the results of such inquiries to help make recommendations for teacher change and can also interpret the work as a signal of good teaching practice. Summatively, accounts of involvement in classroom assessment and research can be submitted by the teacher to the peer reviewer, whose function it is to evaluate this work in terms of what it says about the teacher in comparison with others.

Sometimes, formal teaching scholarship also results in papers, book chapters, seminars, or presentations at professional meetings. Examination of these works or descriptions of the events by the colleague provide the information needed for assessing the contribution. The questions in the resource materials section of this chapter may help in gathering data or evaluating data from papers and book chapters. For formative evaluation, feedback by the reviewer on areas in which the colleague can improve and areas in which the colleague already excels is in order. Summative feedback would result in a written overall assessment of the colleague's performance compared to others in the department or field.

DEPARTMENTAL TEACHING EFFORTS

An important aspect of a faculty member's teaching performance is the extent to which he or she is engaged in collaborative efforts to improve teaching at the departmental, college, or university levels or within the professional associations of the discipline. Such activities might include chairing committees on various aspects of teaching or faculty development, serving in such departmental leadership roles as director of undergraduate or graduate studies, serving as a TA supervisor or mentor to new faculty, or organizing an institute or sessions on teaching at professional association conferences. Information on this work is most likely found in the person's curriculum vitae, but a short interview may help to augment understanding of the activities that have been undertaken and the impact they have had. The questions in the resource materials section may help in gathering data or evaluating data from the curriculum vitae. For formative evaluation, feedback by the reviewer on areas in which the colleague can improve and areas in which the colleague already excels is in order. Summative feedback would result in a written overall assessment of the colleague's performance compared to others in the department or field.

Teaching efforts not captured by classroom observation or review of course materials also are important to peer review. These include such activities as advising undergraduate and graduate students and serving as moderator for a student organization. Again, while these may be considered service rather than teaching, they are an essential part of teaching at almost all institutions, and as such, should be considered when discussing peer review of teaching. *Evaluating Teaching Effectiveness* by Braskamp, Brandenburg, and Ory (1984) is one of the few books that includes a form that can be used to assess such teaching. The resource materials section for this chapter contains another.

Resource Materials:
Leadership for teaching

QUESTIONS FOR ASSESSING QUALITY OF SCHOLARSHIP OF TEACHING

QUESTIONS ABOUT CONTRIBUTIONS TO TEACHING LEADERSHIP EFFORTS

QUESTIONS ABOUT NONCLASSROOM TEACHING

QUESTIONS FOR ASSESSING QUALITY OF SCHOLARSHIP OF TEACHING

Extent of Scholarship

- What evidence is the colleague able to produce on scholarly efforts concerning teaching?
- How does the quantity of these efforts compare with that of other colleagues?

Quality of Scholarship

- Do the papers, presentations, and the like show an examination of the assumptions in the teaching of the field?
- Do the papers provide a framework for analysis of the issues, theoretical or otherwise?
- Are the methods used to explore the question appropriate and used according to the standards of the field?
- Are the conclusions clear and warranted by the evidence or argument?

Impact of Scholarship

- Has the work been endorsed or valued by others, as evidenced by publication in a peer reviewed journal or presentation through invited addresses?
- Has the work been disseminated to others in the department, college, university, or professional group?
- Has the work generated public discussion in the field or inspired students or colleagues to engage in scholarship on the teaching of the discipline?
- Has the work changed the teaching conceptions or practices in the field?

Chism, N.V.N. (1999). *Peer Review of Teaching: A Sourcebook.* Bolton, MA: Anker Publishing Co., Inc.

QUESTIONS ABOUT CONTRIBUTIONS TO TEACHING LEADERSHIP EFFORTS

Extent of Involvement

- With what types of activities has the colleague been involved? (curriculum committee, education special interest group of the professional association, etc.)
- Has the person initiated these efforts personally?
- What role has the person taken in these activities? (chairperson, resource person, etc.)
- To what extent has the person served as a teaching mentor to new faculty or to graduate students in the department?
- How much time does the person devote to these activities compared to other colleagues?

Quality of Involvement

- According to others who have served on committees or other initiatives concerning teaching with the person, has his or her contribution been helpful to the work of the committee?
- Is the person's name known at the departmental, university, or professional levels as one who is a leader with respect to teaching?
- Is the person sought after for projects concerning teaching or for mentoring?

Results of Efforts

- What improvements have resulted from the colleague's work at the deparment, college, university, or professional association?
- Have products or processes developed through the colleague's activities been disseminated?
- What feedback have others provided about the impact of this colleague's work on their teaching?
- What is the overall impact of the colleague's work in this area on teaching at the departmental, college, university, or professional association levels?

Chism, N.V.N. (1999). *Peer Review of Teaching: A Sourcebook.* Bolton, MA: Anker Publishing Co., Inc.

QUESTIONS ABOUT NONCLASSROOM TEACHING

Extent of Involvement

- How involved has the instructor been with respect to undergraduate or graduate student advising?
- Is there evidence that the instructor makes contact with families, employers, and other relevant parties in carrying out advising responsibilities?
- What kind of time commitment does the instructor make to undergraduate and graduate student advising, compared with other instructors in the academic unit?
- Does the instructor participate in seminars, activities, and projects involving students?
- Does the instructor help with efforts designed to attract students to the field?

Quality of Involvement

- Is the instructor sought after as an advisor?
- Do students report that the instructor has been accessible and has supported their progress?
- Does the instructor communicate enthusiasm for the field?

Results of Efforts

- Do students advised by this instructor prosper?
- Is the thesis and dissertation work of graduate students done well?
- Do students advised by this person make progress toward their degrees and obtain employment or seek further academic degrees upon graduation?
- Do students become attracted to work in the field as the result of this person's efforts?

Chism, N.V.N. (1999). *Peer Review of Teaching: A Sourcebook.* Bolton, MA: Anker Publishing Co., Inc.

REFERENCES

Angelo, T., & Cross, P. (1993). *Classroom assessment techniques* (2nd ed.). San Francisco, CA: Jossey-Bass.

Boyer, E. (1990). *Scholarship reconsidered: Priorities of the professoriate.* Princeton, NJ: The Carnegie Foundation for the Advancement of Teaching.

Braskamp, L, Brandenburg, D., & Ory, J. (1984). *Evaluating teaching effectiveness.* Thousand Oaks, CA: Sage.

Chapter 8

Teaching Portfolios

Since the 1980s, teaching portfolios (called dossiers) have been a mainstay of faculty life in Canadian universities. More recently, they have been introduced in the U.S. as a way for faculty to document their teaching, both for improvement and personnel decision-making purposes. A portfolio consists of documents, photographs, videotapes, or other artifacts that describe the teaching of its composer. Teaching portfolios can concentrate on only one course or they may span much longer time periods and teaching situations. The main advantage of a portfolio is that it presents information holistically. A good portfolio is woven together by narrative commentary from the faculty member that describes the context for the documentation and presents reflections on the teaching self. It presents multiple sources of evidence, chronicles the development of the instructor, and projects a future vision.

REVIEWING TEACHING PORTFOLIOS

Peer review of teaching portfolios corresponds to the purpose of the portfolio. When a portfolio is being assembled for formative purposes, the peer reviewer's role is to give advice, not only on teaching development, but on the construction of the portfolio itself. The reviewer can appraise the portfolio through the eyes of others who will ultimately review it for decision-making. The peer is acting in a mentor role in this function, helping the instructor to select those documents that are most descriptive of the teaching as well as reading and providing suggestions on the narrative that the instructor uses to situate the course syllabus, handout samples, summaries of student evaluations, or other items in the portfolio. These conversations are powerful forms of assistance to the faculty member using the portfolio for improvement purposes.

Several institutions use the construction of a portfolio as the occasion for collaborative faculty development. Teachers come together to discuss a given portfolio component, such as syllabi or summaries of student ratings or teaching philosophy statements, for the purpose of common reflections and exploration of assumptions.

When a portfolio is used summatively, the peer reviewer is in the position of making a judgment on the overall quality of the teaching as evidenced by the portfolio. Reviews of teaching portfolios for summative purposes have not been without problems. Several studies point out problems with reliability of ratings. Centra, who did one of the primary studies, concludes (1993) that it is important to consider carefully how reviewers are selected, that the portfolio should include actual work samples rather than only reflective statements or summaries of judgments of others, and that reviewers should receive training in evaluating portfolios according to agreed-upon criteria. Braskamp and Ory (1994) recommend that several colleagues, each using a list of specific criteria, review the portfolio independent of each other. They further make the following recommendations (p. 236):

- Institutional records that are collected periodically and systematically will provide the most comprehensive profiles of performance over the career of a faculty member.
- Actual work samples enhance the authenticity of portfolios.
- Faculty need freedom to organize their records and evidence to reflect their unique contributions. A balance between individuality and campus standardization is necessary.
- Faculty should be given an opportunity to view the results of the document to correct any factual errors.
- Faculty can be given examples of portfolios to help them prepare their own.
- Consultants, especially faculty experienced with portfolios, can help faculty prepare and review their portfolios.
- Guidelines should be provided to course material reviewers to increase interrater reliability.

Although it is important that the academic unit come to agreement on a set of criteria to use in reviewing portfolios, some general criteria can be posed here for consideration.

Completeness

Is the portfolio thorough? Does it contain enough evidence to judge the quality of the teaching? (A list of possible items is in the resource materials section of this chapter.)

Consistency

Do the materials submitted show that there is a match between what the instructor says are goals and the actions taken in teaching? For example, do the statements in the philosophy of teaching correspond with the implicit philosophy in the syllabus, tests, and handouts or in the classroom teaching described on the peer observation record?

Reflection

Does the instructor show a thoughtfulness about teaching through the inclusion of self-evaluation materials, philosophy of teaching statements, goal statements, and commentary on the portfolio documents? Does this reflection offer insights about the context of the documents in the portfolio, about the instructor's efforts to improve, about the vision for the future?

Quality

Does the portfolio show improvement over time? Do the documents and other products portray a teacher whose work is exemplary in the field? Compared to other portfolios, does this portfolio show that students and peers rate the teaching highly? Does the overall portfolio show innovation, experimentation, accuracy of content, and other desirable characteristics?

Credibility and Reliability

Is the assembled evidence well-rounded and detailed, rather than one-sided? Are the judgments of peers, students, and others that are contained in the portfolio documentation in agreement? Is there a balance among the sources of evidence that includes the self, students, and peers?

Examples of systems for evaluating teaching portfolios are in Seldin (1993) and in the resource materials section of this chapter.

Chism, N.V.N. (1999). *Peer Review of Teaching: A Sourcebook*. Bolton, MA: Anker Publishing Co., Inc.

Resource Materials:
Teaching portfolios

POSSIBLE PORTFOLIO ITEMS

REVIEW OF PORTFOLIOS INTENDED FOR IMPROVEMENT PURPOSES

REVIEW OF PORTFOLIOS INTENDED FOR SUMMATIVE PURPOSES *(Narrative Version)*

REVIEW OF PORTFOLIOS INTENDED FOR SUMMATIVE PURPOSES *(Rating Form Version)*

POSSIBLE PORTFOLIO ITEMS

Several books detail the items that can be a part of a teaching portfolio. Lists can be found in Shore, Foster, Knapper, Nadeau, Neill, and Sim (1986), O'Neil and Wright (1993), Murray (1995), and Seldin (1997). The list below contains items that are usually mentioned.

- Description of teaching responsibilities (including advising and other work)
- Statement of teaching philosophy and goals
- Representative course syllabi
- Samples of course handouts and tests
- Self-evaluation statement
- Description of course development or teaching improvement efforts
- Copies of papers or presentations on teaching topics
- Videotape of classroom teaching
- Records of teaching awards and honors
- Summaries of student evaluations of teaching
- Reports of peers who have observed class
- Comments of others who have reviewed course materials
- Comments of those who know about the instructor's teaching contributions to the department or field
- Samples of student work (preferably graded)

REVIEW OF PORTFOLIOS INTENDED FOR IMPROVEMENT PURPOSES

Ideally, feedback on a portfolio that is being compiled for purposes of improvement is exchanged during personal conversations. However, when the reviewer is at a distance or in-person meetings or phone calls are not feasible, written feedback might be the only practical way to respond. The items below are based on the criteria presented earlier (completeness, consistency, reflection, quality, credibility, and reliability) and can be used to prepare to give oral feedback as well as to provide a written response. These items look at the overall portfolio, assuming that the feedback forms presented earlier might be used to assess different components of the portfolio, such as the syllabus and course materials.

1) Does the portfolio contain the type and amount of infor-   **yes**   **no**
mation needed to address the instructor's concerns about
his/her teaching?
If so . . .
   What do the materials tell you about these concerns?

If not . . .
   What other materials would be helpful?

2) Looking over the materials that are assembled, are there clear   **yes**   **no**
connections between espoused intentions (course goal
statements, philosophy statements) and actual practices
(assessment measures, syllabus format)?
If so . . .
   What good connections are in evidence?

If not . . .
   What things need to be aligned?

Chism, N.V.N. (1999). *Peer Review of Teaching: A Sourcebook.* Bolton, MA: Anker Publishing Co., Inc.

3) Does the portfolio contain reflective statements by the instructor   **yes**   **no**
that show engagement with the central teaching issues? Is
there enough context provided so that the reviewer knows
how to evaluate the information?
If so . . .

What are your responses to these reflections?

If not . . .

What questions might the instructor think and write about?

What might help the instructor to be reflective?

4) Is the portfolio organized in such a way as to show   **yes**   **no**
improvement?
If so . . .

What changes do you note?

If not . . .

How can the instructor best improve the organization of
the portfolio to be able to see patterns over time?

5) Has the instructor drawn on other sources of opinion and   **yes**   **no**
evidence in compiling the portfolio?
If so . . .

What patterns do you note across the assembled evidence?

If not . . .

How can the instructor collect multiple kinds of data?

Chism, N.V.N. (1999). *Peer Review of Teaching: A Sourcebook.* Bolton, MA: Anker Publishing Co., Inc.

6) Overall, are there other ways in which the instructor should   **yes   no**
   work with the portfolio concept for the improvement of
   teaching, such as compiling a course portfolio, reviewing and
   revising regularly, or the like?

   If so . . .

   > What recommendations would you make?

7) Are certain items in this portfolio suitable for use in a   **yes   no**
   summative portfolio?

   If so . . .

   > Which ones?

   If not . . .

   > What items would better demonstrate teaching effectiveness when
   > decision-making is the purpose?

REVIEW OF PORTFOLIOS INTENDED FOR SUMMATIVE PURPOSES
(Narrative Version)

In reviewing a portfolio for summative purposes, the focus is not on the process dimensions of assembling a portfolio, but rather on what the evidence says about the effectiveness of the teaching of the portfolio owner and how this compares with the teaching of others. Thus, the review of each of the portfolio components (syllabus, course materials, and the like) should be done individually, using the kinds of instruments in the previous resource section or alternative systematic procedures that the group originates. These evaluations of the individual components form the basis for an overall evaluation.

Prior to the time of a summative portfolio review, instructors should receive clear directions about what the portfolio should contain and how it will be judged. At the time of the review, raters should have standard and systematic procedures for undertaking the review. Traditionally, the review process has consisted of a group conversation, followed by a letter summarizing that conversation. While such narrative feedback may be the option of choice in a given situation, it should be based on articulated criteria and standards. A set of open-ended questions that will guide the reviewer's narrative may help to provide better reliability than this approach has enjoyed to date. The questions might include:

• Does this instructor possess a broad, deep, and current knowledge of the content, as demonstrated by the course syllabi, bibliographies, assignments, handouts, and tests in the portfolio? Is there previous peer testimony about this knowledge through reports of classroom visits, review of materials, or the like?

• Does the instructor use good design principles to facilitate learning in the courses taught, as demonstrated by the teaching philosophy statement and course materials?

• Does the instructor deliver effective instruction, as indicated by summaries of previous student evaluations of instruction, reports by peers, and review of the products of student learning, such as tests, papers, and project reports?

Chism, N.V.N. (1999). *Peer Review of Teaching: A Sourcebook.* Bolton, MA: Anker Publishing Co., Inc.

- Has the instructor shown effectiveness in nonclassroom teaching roles, such as student advising and supervision of student research, as demonstrated by student testimony, student progress, and the products of student learning?

- Does the instructor invest in teaching development and engage in the scholarship of teaching, as demonstrated by the teaching philosophy statement; the record of teaching leadership efforts inside the department and externally; and the record of publication, presentation, and conference participation in the teaching of the discipline?

- Has the instructor contributed extensively to the teaching mission of the department, as indicated by the record of teaching responsibilities, both through formal courses, nonclassroom teaching, and course development?

- Overall, what is the quality of teaching documented in this portfolio and what recommendation do we make on this personnel decision?

Chism, N.V.N. (1999). *Peer Review of Teaching: A Sourcebook.* Bolton, MA: Anker Publishing Co., Inc.

REVIEW OF PORTFOLIOS INTENDED FOR SUMMATIVE PURPOSES
(Rating Form Version)

Instead of a narrative report, reviewers can use a summative rating form that illustrates the judgment process more specifically. The form should originate in discussions within the academic unit about its priorities and standards. To put together such an overall evaluation form, raters must first determine certain things:

- The areas in which the instructor will be assessed
- The evidence that will be used to decide each area
- The relative weight of each of the areas
- The criteria for excellence
- The rating scale

Areas of Teaching and Evidence

The areas should be broad, since an overall assessment is being sought. Portfolio evidence suitable to each area should be listed. Possibilities include:

Evidence of content expertise. To what extent do these materials show that the instructor has a broad, deep, and current knowledge of the content he or she is teaching?

- Course syllabi
- Course reading list/bibliography
- Course assignments
- Course handouts and visuals
- Tests
- Reports of classroom visits by peers

Evidence of instructional design expertise. To what extent does the portfolio show that the instructor uses good design principles to facilitate learning in the courses taught?

- Philosophy of teaching statement
- Course syllabi

Chism, N.V.N. (1999). *Peer Review of Teaching: A Sourcebook.* Bolton, MA: Anker Publishing Co., Inc.

- Course assignments
- Course handouts
- Tests

Evidence of expertise in instructional delivery. To what extent does the instructor deliver effective instruction, both in the classroom and outside?

- Reports of student ratings of instruction
- Reports of classroom visits by peers
- Review of products of student learning (papers, tests, project reports)
- Reports of advisee opinion and progress

Evidence of teaching development and scholarship. To what extent does the portfolio demonstrate that the instructor invests in teaching improvement activities and participates in the scholarship of teaching in his or her field?

- Philosophy of teaching statement
- Report of teaching leadership efforts within the department, institution, professional association, nation, or world
- Record of publication, presentation, and conference participation in the area of teaching within the discipline or generally

Evidence of involvement in teaching. How extensive is the instructor's record?

- Record of teaching responsibilities, including course development
- Record of advising and other nonclassroom teaching responsibilities

Relative Weight of Each Area

A conversation about the value placed on each area identified relative to the whole should result in some consensus about these values. For the above categories, for example, the scheme might look like this:

Content expertise	30%
Instructional design expertise	20%
Expertise in instructional delivery	30%
Teaching development and scholarship	10%
Involvement in teaching	10%

Criteria for Excellence and Rating Scale

Within each category, peers should come to some agreement about what criteria will be used to determine excellence and how these will be reflected in a rating scheme. For the categories in this appendix, for example, the following criteria might be used to assess content expertise.

Content expertise

Factual accuracy	Extremely accurate	Some errors noted	Inaccurate
	3	2	1
Breadth of knowledge	Extremely broad	Somewhat broad	Very narrow
	3	2	1
Depth of knowledge	Extremely deep	Somewhat deep	Very superficial
	3	2	1
Currency	Cutting edge	Somewhat current	Outdated
	3	2	1

Explanatory comments:

Chism, N.V.N. (1999). *Peer Review of Teaching: A Sourcebook.* Bolton, MA: Anker Publishing Co., Inc.

Putting It All Together

When the above have been determined, the final form can contain a tabulation section that lists the areas, the instructor's score for each area, the weight for each area, and the instructor's total score. These scores can then be compared with those of other instructors in making personnel decisions. Context must be considered in making these comparisons. A place for decision rendered is often added. Summary written comments are optional, but desirable. A total section might look like this:

Total

	Instructor's Rating	x	Weight	=	Score
Content expertise	_____	x	.30		_____
Instructional design expertise	_____	x	.20		_____
Expertise in instructional delivery	_____	x	.30		_____
Teaching development and scholarship	_____	x	.10		_____
Involvement in teaching	_____	x	.10		_____

Total score out of a possible_____ points: _____

Comparison to norm/previous scores:

Considerably Higher	Slightly Higher	Average	Slightly Lower	Considerably Lower

Recommendation (promote, salary increase, etc.):

Summary Statement:

Chism, N.V.N. (1999). *Peer Review of Teaching: A Sourcebook.* Bolton, MA: Anker Publishing Co., Inc.

REFERENCES

Braskamp, L., & Ory, J. (1994). *Assessing faculty work: Enhancing individual and institutional performance.* San Francisco, CA: Jossey-Bass.

Centra, J. (1993b). *Use of teaching portfolios and student evaluation for summative purposes.* Paper presented at the annual meeting of the American Educational Research Association, Atlanta, GA. ED 358 133.

Murray, J. (1995). *Successful faculty development and evaluation: The complete teaching portfolio.* ASHE-ERIC Higher Education Report, No. 8. Washington, DC: The George Washington University, Graduate School of Education and Human Development.

O'Neil, C., & Wright, A. (1993). *Recording teaching accomplishment* (4th ed.). Halifax, Nova Scotia: Dalhousie University.

Seldin, P. (1993). *Successful use of teaching portfolios.* Bolton, MA: Anker.

Seldin, P. (1997). *The teaching portfolio: A practical guide to improved performance and promotion/tenure decisions* (2nd ed.). Bolton, MA: Anker.

Shore, B., Foster, S., Knapper, C., Nadeau, G., Neill, N., & Sim, V. (1986). *The teaching dossier: A guide to its preparation and use.* Montreal, Canada: Canadian Association of University Teachers.

Chapter 9

Summary

Although this volume has focused in some detail on the development of systematic processes for peer review of teaching, a primary consideration to the effectiveness of any peer review process is more overarching and less practical—an attitude of professionalism that respects both the individual colleague and the profession of college teaching itself. When peer review is undertaken as an activity that is critical to the well-being of one's profession and one's institution as well as an important opportunity to provide a colleague with developmental direction, it requires certain "habits of the heart":

1. Peer review of teaching must be perceived as a valuable activity, even though it is not directed to one's own specific interests and purposes. It requires an appreciation for a larger mission than one's own in order to devote time to the development of another person and to the quality of one's profession. It also requires the type of vision that enables one to see why this investment is ultimately very important.

2. Peer review of teaching must be seen as both compassionate and principled. Accomplishing the work of college teaching is not easy; there are rigorous standards of performance that must be upheld. On the other hand, helping others appreciate the complexity of teaching and rise to the challenge of teaching well requires patience and understanding.

3. Peer review of teaching requires generosity of spirit. It calls upon the reviewer to put aside rivalries, bad memories, self-interest, and petty likes and dislikes in order to be fair to another. Reviewers also need to be open-minded regarding different approaches; they may need to overlook habits that they find annoying or turf issues that are present as they conduct reviews.

4. Peer review of teaching requires patience and attention to detail. The work of examining graded papers, observing classes, and reading philosophies of teaching might not be highly compelling tasks to most academics, yet in order for peer review to yield good results, these tasks must be done carefully and thoughtfully.

5. Peer review of teaching requires an attitude of intellectual and professional curiosity. This work raises issues that are troublesome for the reviewer, issues such as: What do grades mean? What are the central structures of this discipline? What do students need to know? It is important that a reviewer be able to embrace and struggle with these issues in order to approach the work with the depth it demands as well as to enable growth through the process.

6. Peer review of teaching requires creativity. Especially when used formatively, peer review can be embedded in various situations designed to make it most effective. Asking faculty to identify their favorite and least favorite kind of student opens up windows for exploration; generating new ways of analyzing and presenting data can help colleagues see interesting parallels and contradictions in students' and faculty's comments about their teaching behaviors.

7. Peer review requires courage. It is not easy to be honest with our peers, and it is often uncomfortable to stand in judgment. In the case of summative peer review, consequences of the peer reviewer's decisions can be dramatic. In formative peer review, conversations can touch on issues very sensitive to the colleague and will require honesty and commitment to complete.

8. Peer review requires that reviewers be willing to grow themselves. Evaluating others' work means being open-minded to possibilities and practices that are different from one's own. It necessitates much reflection about criteria and often will call for testing taken-for-granted assumptions and routines in light of differences.

Developing a Set of Principles

Just as it is important to develop peer review practices that set out criteria, activities, and timelines, it is advantageous to think more philosophically about the process as a whole. The "habits of the heart" listed above might serve as a springboard for a given academic unit to discuss its hopes and commitments toward peer review. Although it might be a good exercise to develop this vision at the beginning of peer review activity, lessons learned during the first phases of implementation can add to or inspire such a document and enhance its authenticity.

One sample of a statement comes from the developers of a project on peer review training and education in the College of Letters and Science at the University of Wisconsin, Oshkosh. Professors Baron Perlman and Lee McCann enumerated the following guiding principles for their project on the peer review of teaching.

Guiding Principles for Quality Peer Review of Teaching

Whether a peer review of classroom teaching includes classroom visits, a teaching portfolio, or a more limited submission of teaching materials (e.g., syllabi) there are certain general principles of which to be aware.

1. Knowing and understanding a subject does not mean you can teach it. Good teachers are made, not born.

2. Considerable thought and effort is needed for good peer review. The unit needs to give thought to its criteria and process: The reviewers and those being reviewed will contribute significant time and effort. A review involves gathering data, insight by both reviewer and teacher, and helpful feedback.

3. The notion of "to sit beside" is critical. As described by Braskamp and Ory (1994):

> "To sit beside" brings to mind such verbs as to engage, to involve, to interact, to share, to trust. It conjures up team learning, working together, discussing, reflecting, helping, building, collaboration. It makes one think of cooperative learning, community, communication, coaching, caring, and consultation. When two people "sit beside" each other, engaged in assessing, one may very well be judging and providing feedback about the other's performance, but the style and context of the exchange is critical. "Sitting beside" implies dialogue and discourse, with one person trying to understand the other's perspective before giving value judgments. Describing and understanding precede judging, but consensus is not the goal.

Peer review does not involve a nonexpert consulting with or being acted upon by an expert. The most successful peer review processes of teaching are collaborative. Such peer review involves:

- Helping and building, not judging
- Two professionals working with each other on teaching
- Engagement, collaboration, and reflection
- Dialogue and discourse
- Describing and understanding—the ultimate goal is better teaching

4. Peer review focuses on the thinking behind the work—faculty members' reasons for teaching the way they do, as well as the actual work itself. Teachers being reviewed need to give thought to their approaches to teaching.

5. Good peer review involves being tough on the issues but tender on the person.

6. Unit guidelines and processes must allow for presentation and review of more than classroom teaching: i.e., the advising, supervising, guiding, and

mentoring of students; developing learning activities, such as designing or redesigning courses and unit curricula; and development as a teacher.

7. Discourse is to be based on reasoned options, not personal biases or judgments. A good peer review requires reflection by the reviewees on their teaching and course materials, and by the reviewers on what they have read, discussed, and experienced.

8. Reviewers also benefit from peer review.

9. There should be no surprises. Faculty must know the use to which a peer review will be put. Everyone in a unit must know the process and criteria as clearly set forth. The reviewer and teacher must agree on the process of peer review. Confidentiality in a formative review must be maintained. The literature supports visiting a class, for example, by invitation only. Yes, you may get the teacher's best effort, but since there should be multiple sources of assessment of teaching (e.g., student evaluations, portfolio, materials), the unit will learn if this best effort (assuming it is passable) is representative.

10. Peer review focuses on specific teaching behaviors (e.g., syllabi, handouts, organization of lecture, eliciting questions from students, level of content).

11. Build on strengths. It is easy to pick out what needs work. First identify what went well and only then offer feedback on what might be worked on so the faculty member teaches even better.

12. Feedback must be provided in a timely and thoughtful manner. The reviewer should meet with a faculty member being reviewed to provide this feedback (even when college-wide peer review is ongoing). This conversation should be followed by written feedback when summative review is taking place. Remain available for assistance in the future. Your feedback may be needed again at a later date.

13. Do no harm. Peer review can be anxiety producing and difficult for both reviewer and reviewee. Reviewers may worry that their findings may cause someone to be denied tenure, or be made public and cause dissension and disagreement, and that they were not sensitive enough to the self-esteem and feelings of the faculty member who is being reviewed.

   The person being reviewed, whether for summative or formative purposes, may be concerned about being found wanting, about being less than excellent, or being treated unfairly or harshly.

   Trust and working together minimize the potential for harm and maximize positive outcomes such as better teaching.

14. Be patient. Changing unit or institutional culture and climate towards a systematic peer review process can be slow and difficult. Those being reviewed need time to adjust to the idea and the process. Those doing the reviewing need time to improve their skills and learn how to work with colleagues on teaching-related issues.

15. Peer review takes time. The process is often more time-consuming than other approaches that many faculty are currently using. Yet the sense of contributing to teaching development and working with colleagues usually makes the additional responsibility and time commitment worthwhile. There are no easy answers to the time that peer review takes.

REVIEW

The following steps toward the development of a peer review system have been enumerated in this volume:

1. Obtaining commitment

2. Assigning leadership responsibility

3. Developing a statement that specifies:
 • Who will be included
 • What purposes peer review will serve
 • What areas of teaching will be reviewed
 • What standards will be used
 • How the evidence will be collected
 • What process will be used for assessing the evidence
 • How feedback will be provided/judgments will be documented

4. Developing guiding principles

5. Assigning oversight responsibility

6. Allocating resources

7. Communicating the plan

8. Implementing the system

9. Periodically assessing and revising the system

Peer review provides an opportunity for dialogue and reflection on teaching that not many other activities afford. While it doubtless adds to the time commitments of an already overcommitted faculty, peer review is too important to neglect. As an essential activity directed toward the development of college teachers and the effectiveness of the teaching profession in higher education, peer review must be the cornerstone of future faculty evaluation methods.

USEFUL SOURCES WITH SUBSTANTIAL SECTIONS ON PEER REVIEW OF TEACHING

American Association for Higher Education. (1995). *From idea to prototype: The peer review of teaching (a project workbook).* Washington, DC: American Association for Higher Education.

Arreola, R. (1995). *Developing a comprehensive faculty evaluation system: A handbook for college faculty and administrators on designing and operating a comprehensive faculty evaluation system.* Bolton, MA: Anker.

Bowser, B. (1997). *UNC intercampus dialogues on peer review of teaching: Results and recommendations.* World Wide Web. http://cte.uncwil.edu/et/prev1.htm.

Braskamp, L., & Ory, J. (1994). *Assessing faculty work: Enhancing individual and institutional performance.* San Francisco, CA: Jossey-Bass.

Centra, J. (1993). *Reflective faculty evaluation: Enhancing teaching and determining faculty effectiveness.* San Francisco, CA: Jossey-Bass.

French-Lazovik, G. (1981). Peer review: Documentary evidence in the evaluation of teaching. In J. Millman (Ed.), *Handbook of teacher evaluation,* pp. 73-89. Beverly Hills, CA: Sage.

Hutchings, P. (1996). *Making teaching community property: A menu for peer collaboration and peer review.* Washington, DC: American Association for Higher Education.

Innovative Higher Education. (1996). Special issue: *20* (4).

Journal on Excellence in College Teaching. (1995). Special issue: *6* (3).

Keig, L., & Waggoner, M. (1994). *Collaborative peer review: The role of faculty in improving college teaching.* ASHE-ERIC Higher Education Report, No. 2. Washington, DC: The George Washington University, Graduate School of Education and Human Development.

Leaming, D. R. (1998). *Academic leadership: A practical guide to chairing the department.* Bolton, MA: Anker.

Seldin, P., & Associates. (1995). *Improving college teaching.* Bolton, MA: Anker.

Weimer, M. (1990). *Improving college teaching: Strategies for developing instructional effectiveness.* San Francisco, CA: Jossey-Bass.

Wright, W. A., & Associates. (1995). *Teaching improvement practices: Successful strategies for higher education.* Bolton, MA: Anker.

References

American Association for Higher Education. (1995). *From idea to prototype: The peer review of teaching (a project workbook)*. Washington, DC: American Association for Higher Education.

Angelo, T., & Cross, P. (1993). *Classroom assessment techniques* (2nd ed.). San Francisco, CA: Jossey-Bass.

Arreola, R. (1995). *Developing a comprehensive faculty evaluation system: A handbook for college faculty and administrators on designing and operating a comprehensive faculty evaluation system*. Bolton, MA: Anker.

Batista, E. (1976). The place of colleague evaluation in the appraisal of college teaching: A review of the literature. *Research in Higher Education, 4*, 257-271.

Bernstein, D. (1996). A departmental system for balancing the development and evaluation of college teaching. *Innovative Higher Education, 20*, 241-247.

Bowser, B. (1997). *UNC intercampus dialogues on peer review of teaching: Results and recommendations*. World Wide Web. http://cte.uncwil.edu/et/prev1.htm.

Boyer, E. (1990). *Scholarship reconsidered: Priorities of the professoriate*. Princeton, NJ: The Carnegie Foundation.

Braskamp, L., Brandenburg, D., & Ory, J. (1984). *Evaluating teaching effectiveness*. Thousand Oaks, CA: Sage.

Braskamp, L., & Ory, J. (1994). *Assessing faculty work: Enhancing individual and institutional performance*. San Francisco, CA: Jossey-Bass.

Ceci, S., & Peters, D. (1982). Peer review: A study of reliability. *Change, 14* (6), 44-48.

Centra, J. (1975). Colleagues as raters of classroom instruction. *Journal of Higher Education, 46,* 327-337.

Centra, J. (1993a). *Reflective faculty evaluation: Enhancing teaching and determining faculty effectiveness.* San Francisco, CA: Jossey-Bass.

Centra, J. (1993b). *Use of teaching portfolios and student evaluation for summative purposes.* Paper presented at the annual meeting of the American Educational Research Association, Atlanta, GA. ED 358 133.

Chickering, A., & Gamson, Z. (1987). Seven principles for good practice in higher education. *AAHE Bulletin, 39* (7), 3-7.

Cohen, P., & McKeachie, W. (1980). The role of colleagues in the evaluation of college teaching. *Improving College and University Teaching, 28* (4) 147-154.

Elbow, P. (1980). One-to-one faculty development. In J. Noonan (Ed.), *Learning about teaching.* New Directions for Teaching and Learning, No. 4. San Francisco, CA: Jossey-Bass.

Feldman, K. (1989). Instructional effectiveness of college teachers as judged by teachers themselves, current and former students, colleagues, administrators, and external (neutral) observers. *Research in Higher Education, 30* (2), 137-94.

French-Lazovik, G. (1981). Peer review: Documentary evidence in the evaluation of teaching. In J. Millman (Ed.), *Handbook of teacher evaluation* (pp. 73-89). Beverly Hills, CA: Sage.

Golin, S. (1990). Four arguments for peer collaboration and student interviewing: The master faculty program. *AAHE Bulletin, 3* (4), 9-10.

Gray, P., Diamond, R., & Adam, B. (1996). *A national study on the relative importance of research and undergraduate teaching at colleges and universities.* Syracuse, NY: Syracuse University Center for Instructional Development.

Hutchings, P. (1994). Peer review of teaching: From idea to prototype. *AAHE Bulletin, 47* (3), 3-7.

Hutchings, P. (1996a). *Making teaching community property: A menu for peer collaboration and peer review.* Washington, DC: American Association for Higher Education.

Hutchings, P. (1996b). The peer review of teaching: Progress, issues, prospects. *Innovative Higher Education, 20,* 221-234.

Innovative Higher Education. (1996). Special issue: *20* (4).

Journal on Excellence in College Teaching. (1995). Special issue: *6* (3).

Kane, J., & Lawler, E. (1978). Methods of peer assessment. *Psychological Bulletin, 85,* 555-586.

Keig, L., & Waggoner, M. (1994). *Collaborative peer review: The role of faculty in improving college teaching.* ASHE-ERIC Higher Education Report, No. 2. Washington, DC: The George Washington University, Graduate School of Education and Human Development.

Leaming, D. R. (1998). *Academic leadership: A practical guide to chairing the department.* Bolton, MA: Anker.

Lewis, K. (1988). Using an objective observation system to diagnose teaching problems. In K. Lewis & J. Lunde (Eds.), *Face to face* (pp. 137-157). Stillwater, OK: New Forums Press.

Malik, D. (1996). Peer review of teaching: External review of course content. *Innovative Higher Education, 20,* 277-285.

Massy, W., Wilger, A., & Colbeck, C. (1994). Overcoming "hollowed" collegiality. *Change, 26* (4), 11-20.

Menges, R. (1991). *Why hasn't peer evaluation of college teaching caught on?* Paper presented at the annual meeting of the American Educational Research Association, Chicago, IL. ED 337 106.

Menges, R., & Svinicki, M. (1996). *Honoring exemplary teaching.* New Directions for Teaching and Learning, No. 65. San Francisco, CA: Jossey-Bass.

Millis, B. (1992). Conducting effective peer classroom observations. In D. Wulff and J. Nyquist (Eds.), *To Improve the Academy, 11* (pp. 189-206). Stillwater, OK: New Forums Press.

Muchinsky, P. (1995). Peer review of teaching: Lessons learned from military and industrial research on peer assessment. *Journal on Excellence in College Teaching, 6* (3), 17-30.

Murray, J. (1995). *Successful faculty development and evaluation: The complete teaching portfolio.* ASHE-ERIC Higher Education Report, No. 8. Washington, DC: The George Washington University, Graduate School of Education and Human Development.

Nordstrom, K. (1995). Multiple-purpose use of a peer review of course instruction program in a multidisciplinary university department. *Journal on Excellence in College Teaching, 6* (3), 125-144.

O'Neil, C., & Wright, A. (1993). *Recording teaching accomplishment* (4th ed.). Halifax, Nova Scotia: Dalhousie University.

Pister, K., & Sisson, R. (1993). *The Pister Report: Lessons learned—the aftermath of the report of the task force on faculty roles and rewards in the University of California.* Presented at the first AAHE Conference on Faculty Roles and Rewards, San Antonio, TX.

Quinlan, K. (1996). Involving peers in the evaluation and improvement of teaching: A menu of strategies. *Innovative Higher Education, 20,* 299-307.

Richlin, L., & Manning, B. (1995a). Evaluating college and university teaching: Principles and decisions for designing a workable system. *Journal on Excellence in College Teaching, 6* (3), 3-15.

Richlin, L., & Manning, B. (1995b). *Improving a college-university teaching evaluation system: A comprehensive, developmental curriculum for faculty and administrators* (2nd ed.). Pittsburgh, PA: Alliance Publishers.

Scriven, M. (1973). The methodology of evaluation. In B. Worthen & J. Sanders (Eds.), *Educational evaluation: Theory and practice* (pp. 60-104). Belmont, CA: Wadsworth.

Seldin, P. (1984). *Changing practices in faculty evaluation.* San Francisco, CA: Jossey-Bass.

Seldin, P. (1993). *Successful use of teaching portfolios.* Bolton, MA: Anker.

Seldin, P., & Associates. (1995). *Improving college teaching.* Bolton, MA: Anker.

Seldin, P. (1997). *The teaching portfolio: A practical guide to improved performance and promotion/tenure decisions* (2nd ed.). Bolton, MA: Anker.

Seldin, P. (1998). How colleges evaluate teaching: 1988 vs. 1998. *AAHE Bulletin, 50* (7), 3-7.

Sell, G., & Chism, N. (1988). *Assessing teaching effectiveness for promotion and tenure: A compendium of reference materials.* Columbus, OH: The Ohio State University Center for Teaching Excellence.

Shore, B., Foster, S., Knapper, C., Nadeau, G., Neill, N., & Sim, V. (1986). *The teaching dossier: A guide to its preparation and use.* Montreal, Canada: Canadian Association of University Teachers.

Shulman, L. (1993). Teaching as community property: Putting an end to pedagogical solitude. *Change, 25* (6), 6-7.

Sorcinelli, M. (1984). An approach to colleague evaluation of classroom instruction. *Journal of Instructional Development, 7* (4), 11-17.

Strenski, E. (1995). Two cheers for peer review: Problems of definition, interpretation, and appropriate function. *Journal on Excellence in College Teaching, 6* (3), 31-49.

Weimer, M. (1990). *Improving college teaching: Strategies for developing instructional effectiveness.* San Francisco, CA: Jossey-Bass.

Wright, W. A., & Associates. (1995). *Teaching improvement practices: Successful strategies for higher education.* Bolton, MA: Anker.

Index